Primary school
deputies handbook

Other titles from Pitman include:

Primary school deputies handbook

by
Gareth Thomas

PITMAN
PUBLISHING

PITMAN PUBLISHING
128 Long Acre, London WC2E 9AN

A Division of Pearson Professional Limited

First published in Great Britain 1995

© Pearson Professional Limited 1995

British Library Cataloguing in Publication Data
A CIP catalogue record for this book can be obtained from the British Library.

ISBN 0 273 61607 2

10 9 8 7 6 5 4 3 2 1

Typeset by Northern Phototypesetting Co Ltd, Bolton
Printed and bound in Great Britain by Bell and Bain Ltd, Glasgow

The Publishers' policy is to use paper manufactured from sustainable forests.

Contents

Introduction

The role of the primary deputy as a key member of the school's senior management team (SMT) has become an increasingly crucial one as schools struggle to keep afloat in a culture of continuous change.

It is no longer enough that the deputy treads dutifully behind the headteacher, picking up crumbs of management wisdom. The complexity of primary school management, for even the smallest of schools, means that there has to be a sharing of labour and responsibilities within the SMT. The notion of a collegiate approach to management is becoming widely accepted and with it the adoption, by head and deputy, of areas of responsibility which reflect their personal aptitudes, knowledge and expertise. The pressure is on. Deputies are increasingly expected to come into post with a basket already half filled with management skills and experiences. There is often a further expectation that they will fill the basket within a short period of time.

This book has been written for a wide audience, firstly for classteachers aspiring to the role of deputy headship, for deputies who are new to their post and for experienced deputies who wish to extend their range of school management knowledge and skills. Although the content has been organised in a sequential fashion, 'Preparation for ...', 'Induction into ....', 'Development of ...,' life isn't always as neat as that so the text can be used as a management handbook to be dipped into as needs arise and at a variety points in the deputy's career.

Being an effective, successful deputy has long been recognised as a challenging and difficult goal to attain and although there are opportunities for aspiring and practising deputies to acquire and develop management skills through INSET, shrinking training budgets will inevitably constrain these. Much of the material in the book has been developed for, and used during, management training courses involving experienced deputies and classteachers preparing for the role, and is intended to be as practical as is possible. Although it cannot replace 'live' training it is hoped that the book will supply back-up material for those who have benefited from management courses and provide a set of school management resources for others.

Part I
Preparation

1 Are you ready

'To begin at the beginning ...'

The principle purpose of Part 1 of this book is to: prepare primary classteachers aspiring to deputy headship, equip them with an awareness of the likely demands of the job and bring them to a state of preparedness and increased confidence in moving their career forward.

The first chapter will aim to:

- examine the opportunities, challenges and constraints of deputy headship;

- discover what is expected of primary deputies by others;

- enable the reader to conduct an audit of their skills, knowledge and experience;

- construct an action plan to develop weak or missing areas in their skills, knowledge or experience;

- introduce the 'professional portfolio'.

Opportunities and constraints – losses and gains

What makes some classteachers, often highly effective men and women achieving high levels of job satisfaction, want to move into the role of deputy? Anyone contemplating this radical move is well advised to step back and take an objective look at their motives and the rationale underpinning such a decision.

Asking established deputies what motivated them to make their first application for a deputy's post elicits a wide and fascinating range of responses. Some replies are quite straightforward and made unhesitatingly: 'I always wanted to be a headteacher and it was a means to getting there' or, as with Mount Everest, 'Because it's there'. Others, honest but perhaps not quite what the governors would want to hear, are along the lines of, 'My salary as a classteacher wasn't enough to get mortgage' and, 'The deputy at my school was so awful I thought anybody could do better than that!'

Fortunately, and reassuringly, a high proportion of practising deputies will give thoughtful and considered responses to the 'Why did you do it?' inquiry. It would seem that their principle motivation came from a growing interest in either management, in a context wider than that of the classroom, or in a developing interest in one or more curriculum areas and a desire to be in a position to influence others across the whole school.

There is a belief that we spend our lives exchanging what we have for what we desire. What then is a primary classteacher likely to be exchanging in moving from the familiar, and very often fulfilling, realm of classroom management, close relationships with children and the camaraderie of the staffroom for the quite different role of deputy head? Let us look in more detail at these three aspects of the classteacher's professional life.

First that of classroom manager. Well, there is a considerable degree of correlation here between the strategies and skills developed by an effective classteacher and those needed for the running of a school. The successful management of resources, space and time demonstrated within the microcosm of the class unit should enable the teacher to shift smoothly into a wider management role as the fundamental skills are, to a large extent, transferable. Conversely the teacher who makes a pig's ear of running a classroom will be provided with ample opportunity to create large-scale chaos if promoted to deputy. If, then, a well run, well managed school is a magnified reflection of a successful classroom the move into senior school management will provide endless opportunities and few constraints. For the competent and effective class manager there are likely to be substantial gains and few losses.

The second area where we might want to weigh profit against

loss is around the unique relationship that builds between the primary teacher and her class. Most teachers would agree that the core of their job satisfaction and feelings of professional fulfilment depends on the, often, intense bond that grows between the individual child and teacher and the class itself and teacher. Can this be sustained when a teacher metamorphoses into a senior manager? The reality of the situation is that the introduction of Local Management, i.e. the devolution of budgets into schools away from central funding by the LEA , the rising cost of teachers' salaries combined with a general shrinking of funding for Primary education means that only a minority of primary deputies will be without a class teaching role.

A recent (summer 1994) straw poll of 24 deputies from a range of London LEAs attending a management training course revealed that just three had a 'floating', non-classteaching, role. This contrasts sharply with the picture only two or three years previously when it was usual to find that even in one-form entry schools, having a roll of less than 200 pupils, deputies would not have a class responsibility.

To return to the question of the loss of the special relationship between teacher and class. It is evident that unless the deputy headship rests within a fairly large primary, at least two-form entry, then the issue is not going to arise. What is likely to be presented are the tensions and constraints generated by having the dual role of classteacher and senior manager. We will be examining this difficult issue later when looking at the role of the deputy.

The third aspect of the teacher's professional life is one which links with their relationships with colleagues, both teaching and non-teaching, and the changes which may arise from the move into senior management. It would be naive to imagine that these relationships won't change, and risky to ignore their consequences. The camaraderie and solidarity of the staffroom, which so often nourishes and supports the classteacher, professionally, emotionally and socially, will inevitably be shifted away from the new deputy. This issue creates particular difficulties for the internally appointed deputy who perhaps carries with them a substantial history as a classteacher in the school and has had long and close friendships within the staff group. For the majority of teachers the change of role and status will mean losses and may introduce interpersonal tensions which will have to be dealt with. A later chapter will examine more closely the intricate relationship between deputy and colleagues and the delicate balancing act that the deputy will have to perform as senior manager and fellow teacher.

We have been looking, briefly, at just three facets of a primary teacher's working life and the potential opportunities, constraints, losses and gains attached to a move into senior management. A useful exercise for those contemplating such a change in role is to draw up a balance sheet for each important aspect of their job before making any final decisions. These could include:

- relationships with parents;
- family and personal commitments;
- curriculum interests;
- union activities;
- cross LEA involvements;
- extra curricula activities.

Readers will be able to add many others from their own agendas and perhaps produce a composite balance sheet which will inform the direction in which they will move and whether the time is right for such a move.

Expectations

It cannot be over emphasised that there are huge expectations and hopes coming from numerous quarters on the appointment of a new deputy. Within the school the headteacher will be anxious to replace a much valued partner in the senior management team or conversely will be desperate to find someone who will be able to compensate for particular areas neglected by the previous post-holder. Teaching and non-teaching colleagues will similarly be viewing the change with a range of overt and hidden agendas. Governors too will have a wide variety of aspirations depending on where in the arena they are standing.

Looking across the wider educational community we find a range of perceptions of what deputy headship is about and here are a selection of views on the purpose and potential of the role which might provide food for thought for the aspiring deputy:

- 'Heads in the making.' (NAHT.)
- 'A dogsbody with poor job satisfaction.' (Welsh HMI, 1985.)
- 'Nearly all deputies should be on the way towards becoming heads.' (Improving Primary Schools, ILEA, 1985.)
- 'This post is of major importance in the primary school because of the high expectations of everyone involved.' (Coulson and Cox, 1975.)

- 'Nearly two-thirds of the deputies were satisfied or very satisfied with their jobs.' (*Schools Matter*, Peter Mortimer.)

- '... take over and fill in for anybody, be it head or dinner helper, so that the school can tick over without others noticing or suffering ... being able to cope.' (ILEA deputy.)

and finally, not totally seriously,

- 'A mouse training to be a rat.' (anon.)

Within each of these comments lies a grain of truth and some aspects of reality. It is unsurprising that there are contradictions and differing perceptions for no two schools and no two deputy headships are ever going to be the same. Teachers contemplating the role are well advised to prepare themselves to be able to match a wide range of demands and a variety of expectations and to investigate as thoroughly as is possible what they are likely to be within the context of a particular school.

Making a professional audit

Having made a thorough assessment of the challenges, opportunities and threats involved in taking on deputy headship, the classteacher will need to review the extent of their accumulated skills and experience and from this create an action plan for further development which will prepare them for the move forward.

We can usefully apply the model used widely in School Development Planning to structure the process. This is represented as a cycle which looks something like that shown in Figure 1.1

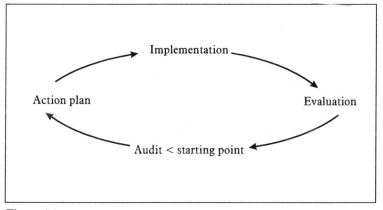

Figure 1.1

The four phases of the cycle represent;

1. **Audit:** the teacher reviews his or her strengths and weaknesses.

2. **Action plan:** professional development priorities are selected and made into targets for action.

3. **Implementation:** priorities and targets are acted upon.

4. **Evaluation:** the outcomes of implementation are assessed.

By its nature the process is ongoing and can provide a helpful tool for self-development throughout a teacher's professional life.

But how to get started?

One method is to compile an inventory of skills, knowledge and experience widely accepted as desirable from a teacher prior to appointment as a deputy and for the individual to compare this with their personal catalogue of achievements.

The reader may find it interesting to complete the check-list presented in Figure 1.2. This has been adapted from a review of the management training needs of aspiring Primary deputies carried out by a team from the National Development Centre at Bristol University. It carries a health warning in that it is essentially a list of items for which management training should be available and not necessarily a menu that teachers will be able to put together without external support. However, it does provide a practical framework for making a personal, professional audit.

So, how are you doing so far?

Run through the check-list and mark each item with *'fully'*, *'partially'*, or *'not at all'*.

In tackling a questionnaire of this sort the value of the exercise can be enhanced by sharing its completion with a 'critical friend'; that is someone with whom one has a professional relationship and who can be trusted to give an honest and objective view of the outcomes. An effective way of doing this is to give the critical friend a copy of the audit questionnaire and ask them to complete as much of it as is practical, naturally using yourself as the subject, and later, comparing this with your own assessment.

Remembering that we have attached a health warning to this exercise, a broad personal assessment can be made by looking at the outcomes of the task;

Professional skills

Have you experienced:

- Successful classteaching across a range of year groups, preferably in more than one school?
- Working to a job description?
- Collaborative or team-work with colleagues, students, primary helpers, etc.?
- Assessing pupils' progress and using formal record keeping systems?
- Curriculum leadership, possibly in more than one area?
- Developing a sound overview of National Curriculum requirements across appropriate Key Stage(s)?
- Comprehensive knowledge and understanding of the NC in one or more curriculum areas?
- Formulating and evaluating schemes of work?
- Implementing school-based INSET?
- Working with parents?
- Co-ordinating and running a school event, i.e. concert, school journey?
- Taking assemblies?

Personal skills

Can you:

- Provide leadership of, and contribute to professional discussion?
- Negotiate effectively?
- Delegate tasks?
- Plan and work as a group member?
- Demonstrate flexibility with other adults?
- Communicate effectively with both children and adults?
- Cope with stress and perform well under pressure?
- Solve problems and act decisively?

Administration experience

Have you experienced

- Report writing?
- Minute taking?
- Requisitioning and monitoring equipment?
- SEN statementing procedures?
- Formal letter writing and telephoning on school's behalf?
- Budgeting and account keeping

Knowledge of external agencies

Do you have:

- Liaison with local schools and the community?
- Awareness of training opportunities and Teachers' Centre activities?
- Understanding of LEA structure and support provision, i.e. educational psychological service, advisory teams, etc.?
- Awareness of provision available for newly qualified teachers (NQTs)?

Figure 1.2

Evaluation

- If the responses have predominantly lain in the area of 'fully met' with a sprinkling of 'partially' and very few 'not' then it can safely be assumed that according to these criteria of readiness the time could be right to start moving forward.

- If there is a balance between the three responses with a leaning towards 'partially' and 'not' then the aspiring deputy will need to take stock and perhaps defer making immediate decisions.

- Certainly if the outcome demonstrates that a substantial number of gaps are showing across the board then serious attention must be given to further professional development before a move forward can be considered

Action planning

Having completed the review of professional skills and competencies and analysed the results a picture will be emerging of areas that may need developing, perhaps with quite specific foci. A helpful way forward at this juncture is the construction of a personal action plan.

The starting point is to list the gaps in experience, skills or knowledge which have been highlighted by the self-evaluation exercise and then try to link these into areas which have a common theme or broad focus. The objective being to plan an activity, undertake a study or set up an experience which will enable several 'gaps' to be covered. This can be best illustrated by looking at a case study.

Case study

Angie P has, with the support of a critical friend, completed the self-evaluation questionnaire and has come up with a profile which looks positive and encouraging. However, it has thrown up several areas which will need developing and she has decided to prepare an action plan which will extend over two terms to deal with the issues.

Her shopping list of concerns are prioritised to:

- involvement with developing schemes of work;

- acting as a team leader;

- implementing INSET;

- assessment and record keeping.

cont.

---

cont.

In order to widen her experience of these areas and to bring them together into a cohesive whole she comes up with the following objective;

'Within her brief as curriculum leader for science, she will establish a curriculum team who, under her leadership will revise existing schemes of work for science, and devise an assessment and recording system appropriate for the subject.'

On achieving this objective she will use a whole-school INSET day to promote and disseminate the outcomes. She discusses her plan with her headteacher who gives it full approval and then sets about structuring a detailed action plan.

We will shortly examine a systematic method for producing the action plan but first let us return to the process that Angie evolved to deal with her professional development needs.

Teachers who are engaged in appraisal schemes will have observed a resonance between elements of the case study and their own experiences of the appraisal process. For example early in the appraisal cycle comes an activity known as self-appraisal which in many respects is identical to the self-evaluation that has been described; the role of critical friend parallels that of appraiser and the setting of targets within teacher appraisal reflects our action planning. From this it is clear that teacher appraisal could well provide the vehicle for teachers moving towards deputy headship within which they may put together a personal development plan. In making this suggestion it must be said that there are logistical problems which will impose constraints on using the appraisal process. For instance, the two-year span of the cycle won't necessarily match the individual teacher's objectives or the school's own Development Plan will have requirements laid on each teacher's targets which will not reflect their personal aims.

To return to the case study. Having defined an overall objective, gained support of senior management and, most importantly, discussed the goals with a critical friend who will then be asked to monitor the action plan, it is time to write a detailed plan.

The plan must be SMART:

Specific
Measurable
Achievable
Realistic
Time constrained.

This acronym is a helpful reminder and provides the elements of the plan. We need to define clearly what is going to be achieved, how we are going to assess that we have reached these goals and what the time frame for completion will be. It can be helpful to break the time element down into short-, medium- and long-term targets. Many teachers have found it useful to produce their action plan in a tabular form as shown in Figure 1.3.

	Personal action plan		
	Within the next few days (short term)	By............ (medium term)	By............. (long term)
I shall myself...			
With others I shall...			
The resources I shall need...			

Figure 1.3

Professional portfolios

During the past three or four years a number of LEAs and HE institutions, in particular the South Bank Polytechnic in London, have been investigating the notion of the 'professional development portfolio'.

A portfolio is simply a device for recording and documenting professional experiences, responsibilities and achievements throughout a teacher's career. Some LEAs have introduced the concept to NQTs so that it becomes an integral part of their induction period.

It is also becoming common to find that higher education institutions will offer Accreditation for Prior Learning (APL). Prior learning can include INSET as well as work-based experiences. These, in turn, may attract accreditation towards components of further qualification such as an Advanced Diploma in Professional Studies or an MA. A carefully compiled portfolio can serve as evidence of learning arising from past experience and in addition contribute usefully in future job applications.

Constructing a portfolio
The framework of a professional portfolio should provide scope for a range of experience and achievements and allow for reflection on them. There is no proscribed format but the shape that seems to emerge generally looks something like this:

1. Career history:
   - CV.
   - Employment record.
   - Professional development activities: courses attended, further qualifications gained, etc.
   - Job descriptions (past and present).

2. Current teaching file:
   - Class responsibility.
   - Curriculum responsibilities.
   - Whole school activities.

3. Teacher appraisal documentation:
   - Record of process.
   - Data collection.
   - Outcomes.
   - Targets and action plans.

4. Reflective writing:
   - Specific projects and tasks
   - Evaluation of curriculum development or policy implementation.

The materials that are gathered need not necessarily be confined to written evidence but could include a variety of media. For example, audio or video cassettes of performances and school productions, or photographic records of class projects and school journeys. A well developed, reflective portfolio will provide valuable material for the aspiring deputy in assessing whether or not the time is right to move on. But for those at other stages in their career, it can provide an opportunity to start gathering together and documenting the accumulated experiences of their professional life.

Summary

This chapter has examined the early stages of the preparation for primary deputy headship, and for teachers at this stage in their career it has made the following recommendation for action:

- to take a careful and wide ranging stock of their personal

and professional situation and to make a balance sheet of
gains and losses;

- to match their own aims and objectives with the expectations held for deputies;

- to conduct a personal audit of their skills, knowledge and experience;

- to construct an action plan to deal with their resulting professional development needs;

- to consider building a professional portfolio.

2 Moving forward

Inevitably, for those who so desire it, the time for moving into senior management will arrive. When, where and how this point is decided upon will be determined by the individual teacher's situation. It is worth remembering that this step is taken only after careful reflection and after the kind of self-assessment suggested in Chapter 1.

This chapter will deal with the processes and procedures that will assist the aspiring deputy in reaching the objective of 'The post that's right for me'.

We will, in a sequential fashion, look at the stages which are necessary to go through to make this a successful career move. These steps are not exclusive to the move to deputy headship but can be equally applied by teachers going for posts of responsibility and, to some extent, for deputies going forward into headship.

The stages will be:

- action planning;
- targeting the schools;
- preliminary visits;
- effective applications;
- interview procedures;
- presentations.

Action planning

These two words will keep cropping up throughout this book; they simply mean achieving an objective through setting targets then constructing a set of actions, set within a time frame, in order to reach these targets.

So, having decided that they are ready for the move and having perhaps spent time in developing some of the weaker areas in their portfolio of skills, knowledge and experience the aspiring deputy will set about writing an action plan.

This will have a time structure within which are a set of targets to be reached. These targets will depend entirely on individual circumstances but could look something like this example:

> **Objective:** To be appointed as deputy head.
> **Proposed deadline:** Mid-point Summer Term 96 (present date September 1995).
> **Targets:**
> – Autumn Term 95 – complete 20-day Maths course, start doing some reading around school management, apply for 'Preparation for Deputy Headship course', set up maths curriculum team.
> – Spring Term – run series of maths workshops, attend preparing for deputyship training at Institute, subscribe to *TES*, make contact with local Primary Deputies support group, use non-contact time to observe own deputy, start making applications after half term.
> – Summer Term – continue making applications, keep up to date with current developments through reading.

It can be seen that this kind of forward planning enables a gradual build up towards the objective and avoids the, more common, situation of being thrown headlong and ill-prepared, into the application process. If the Summer Term does not produce results then the action planning can be shifted forward into the Autumn. The value of action planning is always greatly enhanced by sharing it with a second person, perhaps a colleague whose opinions you value. The peer pressure that this can bring to bear will keep the action planner on her toes! Writing down the action plan in a structured way also helps and an example of a framework that is commonly used was given in Chapter 1 (page 12).

Targeting schools

What are the factors that come to bear on us and influence our actions when applying for teaching posts?

The most obvious, and perhaps the starting point for most people are the personal ones. How far away is it from home? How much time am I going to spend travelling? Am I going to be able to manage the logistics of organising my own children? The nature of the catchment area of the school or the reputation of the LEA will influence some people while the perceived philosophy of the schools themselves will provide the first priority for many teachers.

From the professional perspective it is prudent to consider the special characteristics of the school and how well these match the applicant's previous experience. Aspects of the school worth considering in terms of matching are: its organisation, i.e. infant only, primary or junior only, whether it is county, voluntary aided, or even grant maintained, and the number of children on roll. The way in which the classes themselves are organised will be of crucial importance to others for example whether there is family grouping, whether the building is open planned, whether or not there is collaborative or team teaching.

Information gathering

But, unless the school is already known to us how does the applicant gain a true picture of the school? The usual procedure when looking for a new post is, of course, to scan the educational press to find out what appointments are coming up. These advertisements, formally funded by the relevant local authority, have in the past given a fairly detailed description of the school and the post being advertised. Unfortunately since the delegation of budgets to schools, including the responsibility for advertising, there has been a marked reduction in scope in the content of individual advertisements. To counterbalance this schools now send prospective applicants a comprehensive information pack. This will consist, at a minimal level, of an application form, a person and job description and a description of the school's organisation. Most schools in fact supplement these with a copy of the parents' booklet, the school's or LEA's Equal Opportunities policy and a copy of the LEA's Schoolteachers Pay and Conditions document. This literature, together with data that may be gleaned through networking with teachers working at the school, should provide a comprehensive portrait of the school. If individuals working within the school are known to the prospective applicant then caution needs to be taken in receiving anecdotal information about any school as there is always the danger that this may produce a one-dimensional picture, maybe emphasising warts rather that beauty spots.

Preliminary visits

Headteachers appear to have mixed feelings about allowing whole-sale visiting of applicants to their schools. In some cases this is understandable as the number of applicants for desirable posts may be overwhelming and applicants are only invited in after being short-listed. However as a general rule the applicant has every right to ask for a preliminary visit to the school.

What then are the objectives of this visit and how may they be reached?

Forward planning is important. The preparation of a set of relevant questions before visiting will provide a good starting point. These might cover issues such as the school's current School Development Plan, the school's management structure, control and discipline policies or the role of governors. More pertinent questions relating to the new Deputy's role will need to be raised, and issues such as the curriculum areas for which responsibility will be held.

The time spent at the school will need to be maximised in order to soak up as much of the school's culture, or ethos, as possible. Timing arrival to coincide with a playground period will enable the visitor to gain valuable first impressions, for it is here that the iceberg of the 'hidden curriculum' breaks through the surface. How do children relate to each other, to adults, to strangers? Time with the established teachers in the staffroom is well spent. What overt and covert messages about the school are being given? What is the nature of discussion, does it focus on reading ages, or wallpaper and TV programmes such as *East Enders*? How 'open' is conversation? How are strangers welcomed? Does your observation match what the head has been telling you? And finally spend as much time as possible with the class that will be allocated to the successful applicant.

Preparing the application

The job application is the applicant's first point of contact with the small group who will be making the initial short-listing for interviews. It is absolutely essential that the application procedure is followed carefully according to the guide-lines that accompany the application's documentation. In times of stability, or some would say stagnation, in the teaching jobs market, it is not unusual to find that each deputy post advertised attracts a large field of candidates. With this level of competition and the corresponding amounts of paperwork to be dealt with by appointment committees a strategy often adopted is to weed out the incomplete, or incorrectly filled in applications in order to simplify the process. Unlike other professions teachers are rarely asked to provided a formal CV though it is extremely useful to put one together for your own use. Working back through one's job history for every job application searching for dates and places can be a very time consuming exercise.

The importance of the 'look' of the written application cannot be over-emphasised. An attractive handwriting style needs demonstrating but for others having any doubts about legibility then word-processing is the salvation. Careful spell-checking can also gain some Brownie points.

At the heart of the written application, and the key to its success, will be the response made to the requirements laid out in the job description. This paper may come under a variety of headings: person or job specifications, or sets of 'Essential' and 'desirable criteria'. However they are headed these contain the core items that need to be addressed in the written response. It is fairly usual to have the length of this statement limited to, say, 200 words. If there is no such limit care must be taken to avoid long-windedness and to aim for clarity and conciseness.

There is a current trend, which has developed from the commitment many LEAs and schools now have towards equal opportunities in employment, of setting out a list of essential criteria to which the applicant is asked to respond. An example of such a paper is in Appendix I.

Using a systematic structure like this enables a fairer assessment to be made of each application as the responses should all focus on the same issues. It also provides a set of topics on which the interview questions will be based. But what are the most effective ways of responding to these requirements? First it is critical that each criterion is addressed. There are two possible approaches in dealing with essential criteria. The first is to mechanically move through the list responding to each in turn. This certainly ensures that each topic has been covered but may prevent the writer from putting across any of their personality or style. The second strategy is to carefully structure a 200-word piece of prose which will include references to each of the criteria.

One model for this writing is to construct it in three paragraphs. Then, writing within the context of the post being applied for and the given criteria, paragraph one will *summarise past experience,* the second will demonstrate the applicant's *thinking on current issues in primary education* and the final paragraph will outline *what the applicant considers s/he can bring to the job.*

A tactic, helpful to the short-list group, is to label statements in the text that refer to particular essential criteria with its 'E' number. For example:

'During the past two years I have led and built up a team of
teachers and parents whose purpose has been to involve the
wider parent body in support of teachers in the classroom. (E7,
E8.)'

There are two further points to remember when compiling this piece
of writing. One is that it is the applicant's one shot at getting across
their personality, beliefs and values, and, second that statements and
references made here will probably be taken up at interview. So great
care must be taken with 'trade descriptions'!

Other issues needing care at this stage include ensuring that all
the completed paperwork is returned before the published deadline,
selection panels do stick to deadlines, also that referees must be
approached, and their support confirmed, well before they are likely
to be contacted by the prospective school or LEA: some fundamental actions which if neglected can have costly consequences.

Interview procedures and skills

A surprising number of teachers move through the first stages of
their professional life without having to cope with a formal interview only facing the event for the first time at the interview for
deputy headship. A few may have had experience as teacher governor of being on the other side of the table, but most applicants will
be interview novices filled with misapprehension and anxiety over
what to expect. This section will hopefully illuminate this dark
corner and help provide some confidence for the noviciate.

A good starting point is developing the awareness that those on
the interviewing panel will also be having feelings of anxiety and
stress. The effectiveness of their management, and conduct of the
interview and its successful outcome will have a crucial bearing on
their school for years to come. The interview panel wants the right
person as much as each applicant wants the post.

Before the interviews commence the panel will have been at
work reviewing the process, preparing the questions and deciding
on who will ask them. The standard procedure is to prepare six or so
questions, each of which will closely match a selection criterion,
some to include more than one. Each question will be allocated to
someone on the panel who has a particular interest, or expertise on
that topic. For instance, a question relating to liaison with parents
will naturally fall to one of the parent governors. During each interview the questions will be given in the same form to each interviewee, followed by a supplementary question which will reflect the
response that has been given. Another common practice is for the
questions to be listed on a proforma together with the essential cri-

teria they refer to, and for each of these sheets to be used by panel members to record the individual's response to questioning. These papers may also be collected at the end of interviewing and kept as a record of the proceedings in the event of dispute or complaint by interviewees.

Being interviewed

We have, one hopes, moved a long way from the personnel officer's cynical adage that the majority of job applicants got, or failed to get, appointed during the time it took to walk from the door to their seat. Nevertheless first impressions do count and some forethought before attending an interview will not be wasted time. Firstly the interviewee will have gained some impression from their preliminary visit of the dress code for staff. Bear this in mind when preparing for the interview and always err on the formal side. The governors see staff appointments as one of their most important functions and will themselves regard the occasion with a degree of formality. It is prudent that the applicant reflects this. As the chair of governors makes the introductions a positive gambit is to look each panel member in the eyes and to smile as warmly and convincingly as nerves allow. It is customary for the Chair to offer an unthreatening warm-up question to help the candidate relax. The questioning will then begin according to the panel's pre-arranged plan.

In responding to questions it is worth trying to internalise the following strategies:

- It is all right to pause and reflect on the question before answering.

- If the question is unclear to you, or if it is complex with a number of sub-questions, ask for clarification or to have the question broken down into its component parts. (This kind of question displays a poor technique on the part of the questioner.)

- Whenever possible refer to your practical experience or to reading you have done.

- Be concise and indicate when you have finished your answer.

- Summarise long or complex responses.

- Use a notepad to jot down the salient points of each question before responding.

- Don't invent, if you haven't a clue say so!

- Whenever appropriate, try to make the panel smile.

These can be practised in advance of the interview using a 'critical friend' as an interrogator. This dry-run can be organised fairly easily as the areas of questioning will be defined by the list of essential criteria and there should be few surprises in their content

There are a number of areas of questioning which should be out of bounds according to good equal opportunities practice. These cover the applicant's sexual orientation, marital status, family commitments, political affinities, and religious convictions. The latter though, for obvious reasons, may be discussed during interviews for posts at voluntary-aided schools. Having said this there will be governors who are not as aware of these boundaries as they ought to be and who will slip in inadmissible questions. Good chairing should intervene at this juncture but if this doesn't happen the candidate may gently point out that the question is out of order.

The prepared questions will eventually run their course and the candidate will be faced with the final 'Now, do you have any question you'd like to ask the panel?' There may well be points which have arisen that need clarifying but the advice here is not to ask an extraneous question just for the sake of it and not to ask questions which are beyond the remit of the interviewing panel. It is much better to thank the panel for a stimulating half hour and to withdraw gracefully.

The presentation

As the role of the senior management team has been increasingly seen as one of the critical factors in the running of an effective primary school so has the importance attached to appointing a successful and effective deputy. Governors now regard finding the right person as one of the most influential actions they may perform. The stakes are high. A poor appointment can drag the school down from the achievements it has made or prevent it from moving forward in implementing positive change. The appointment of a strong, effective deputy has also rescued some schools from the consequences resulting from weak headship. So interview practices have become more rigorous and searching and other selection strategies are being introduced to help ensure the right person gets the job. One of the practices which has become fairly widespread is the inclusion of a 'presentation' during the interview, a device which has been used widely in the past for headship appointments. The presentation is simply a time slot allocated to each candidate during which they are asked to talk on a given topic. This short period of time, usually for practical reasons five minutes or so, is regarded by many people with dread. The following advice is given to enable candidates to approach the task with strategies which enable them to better project their thinking and personality.

First it is helpful to clarify the rationale behind the setting of the task. The purpose of the interview presentation is to demonstrate the candidate's ability to:

- perform under pressure;
- think and communicate clearly and concisely;
- express informed views.

Understanding these points will make the task more meaningful and enable us to bring it into focus more clearly.

The normal procedure is for the candidates to be given a topic to work to and a period of time to prepare before their interview. In some situations they are invited to prepare some kind of visual aid to support the presentation. The theme is usually in a fairly predictable area, often linked to the job description or essential criteria. Typical topics might include:

- working with governors;
- school communication;
- managing budgets;
- staff development;
- working with parents;
- running meetings;
- role of the deputy.

The task for the candidate, then, is to communicate their knowledge, experience and views in as interesting, lively and informed a way as is possible. Five minutes may appear to be a daunting void of time to fill but it is in reality a short period in which to put across all that the presenter might want to say. The preparation time must be used effectively, it will probably only be 20 minutes to half an hour. The presentation will need to be carefully structured as the candidate's ability to manage time will be noted by the panel, and be kept to rigidly.

A possible structure for the presentation, which could be applied to a number of the likely topics, might look like this, having three sections:

1. The opportunities offered by the topic.
2. The problems/threats that need to be overcome.

3. The candidate's own experiences relating to these and the
   ideas and views that they have developed.

It is helpful for both the presenter and the interviewing panel to
have the key issues within the talk to be displayed either on a flip
chart or OHP. The presenter will in addition have these headings
broken down further on their notes.

What candidates find most difficult though is not the preparation and finding ideas to talk about but having to deliver the talk
itself to a group of strangers. The following tips, which can be trans-
ferred to many other presentation situations, such as addressing
groups of parents, running whole staff, INSET, etc., may alleviate
some of the angst that is felt by many people.

When having to make a formal presentation:

- dress to feel confident;

- be well prepared;

- at the start; establish eye contact, focus on the friendliest
  face, start with a quotation, bold statement, or even a joke;

- state purpose and outline the structure of the talk;

- have OHTs clearly numbered;

- have notes written boldly on cards, or in large print on
  several sheets of paper;

- at the end; summarise key points and thank listeners for
  their attention.

It is not the usual practice for the panel to ask questions after the
presentation though there could well be reference to what has been
delivered during the course of the interview. Bearing this in mind it
is well for the candidate to include only facts and views that they are
confident in handling.

This brings us to the end of our look at the procedures which will
take the aspiring deputy to the point of waiting for the phone call
which will relay the exciting news of their new appointment.

It is worth reflecting, though, that relatively few will be moved
forward at the first interview and some may well see themselves
facing the selection process several times before the one that is right
for them comes along. Each unsuccessful bid must be used to extract
all the learning that can be gleaned from it. For instance, it is per-
fectly in order to ask, whoever the appropriate person is, head, chair
or inspector, for an interview debriefing. Careful note must be taken
of their comments and areas of weakness identified for working on
before the next application. Discussing these with a colleague or

line-manager can be more fruitful than self-analysis alone, and asking for a candid opinion of the points that have been put in the debriefing will enhance the self-development process.

Many primary management courses include training in interviewing and presentation and provide a useful forum for participants to practice the techniques in a 'safe' unthreatening setting.

3 Basic management Managing yourself and managing with people

Even before the point of contemplating the move to a senior management role is reached the classteacher will have had numerous opportunities to practice personal and people management within their professional life. The organisational, administrative and specialist demands made by the National Curriculum have meant that few teachers, even those newly qualified, will not have had an organisational or leadership role within one or more curriculum areas as a curriculum leader. The importance attached to the role of curriculum leader, or co-ordinator was highlighted in Professor Alexander's, 'Three Wise Men', consultative paper (DES, 1992) and can be seen reflected weekly in primary teaching post advertisements in the press.

Some of these areas will, then, be of importance to both the curriculum leader and the potential deputy. They are fundamental processes and skills necessary for the effective management of all schools and we will now examine in detail:

1. Policy writing.

2. Managing meetings.

3. Time management.

Policy writing

All well run, effective, primary schools have always had policies. Policies to proscribe the delivery of curriculum areas, to define assessment procedures, to describe and provide boundaries for good behaviour and discipline, to outline relationships with parents and the community, to manage the playground, the list is seemingly endless. An important difference between now and the not too distant past is that policies have to be seen, not just in practice, but in document form, in black and white. Whereas it was once acceptable, and widely practiced, that, some school policies, non-curricula policies in particular, could be left unwritten. They would live under the surface of the school's culture or ethos, providing guidance and influencing actions. However, the development of accountability has rendered this *laissez faire* approach out moded. The demands of the OFSTED inspection, the Parent's Charter and the increasingly high political profile of education has created a pressing need for many schools to produce, or update, a multitude of written policies.

Schools faced with this widescale policy review will have to manage an awesome extra workload and this section has been written in the hope that those having to meet the task will come away with the feeling that it is 'do-able'.

We will look at:

● clarifying what makes a policy;

● structuring a policy;

● a policy writing process model.

When is a policy not a policy? Defining the task

As a newly appointed deputy the writer was involved in a pre-inspection school policy review and, as there was no one else willing to do it, was delegated the task of writing a science policy. This had to be produced, as a completed document, during the two-week Easter holiday. What was the process to be? I had no previous experience in policy development, the school had nothing in its archives and the LEA was one which believed in a hands off approach to curriculum matters in general. My approach was, I suspect, a fairly typical one for that period. Gathering together all the science texts I could find in the school, and using my limited range of classroom science practice I cobbled together a set of activities, a compendium of resources and a set of targets for each year group to achieve. The document, duly typed by the school secretary, was accepted unquestioningly by head and staff and was immediately put away into desk drawers where it probably still lies, unlooked at and unloved.

This anecdote is given to serve as an illustration of what a written policy should not be and how not to do it. What had been produced was a crude programme of study, there had been no involvement with others in its production and it was destined to produce no discernible change within the school.

Much of what follows is based on a model of policy development presented by Brian Caldwell and Jim Spinks in *The Self-Managing School* (1988); ideas which have had considerable influence within primary school management training over recent years.

A useful starting point is to consider '*Why have written policies?*' For it is undeniable that policy writing consumes time, energy and possibly other valuable resources. Badly managed policy development may lead to contention, confrontation and encourage negativity. If faced with large scale policy review, and particularly in a school which has not had a culture of collaborative working, a helpful exercise is to brain-storm, as a staff group, this very question.

The result of this task will generally produce a list of benefits which closely matches that found in Hargreaves and Hopkins' *The Empowered School* (1991).

Written policies will:

- provide explicit links between aims (goals) and action;

- give unambiguous guides for action, ensuring consistency between teachers in operating the policy;

- save time and avoid confusion and conflict;

- allow the school to check consistency between policies;

- ease the induction of new staff;

- help the school to explain to its partners what it is doing, and why;

- support planning, since sound policies are part of the maintenance system, and poor policies or lack of policy becomes a priority for development.

This exercise can provide a way forward in dealing with colleagues whose previous experiences of policy writing and implementation have not been positive but, of course, it is not being suggested that it need be applied to all staff groups.

Let us try and clarify what a policy should be, remembering that the science paper mentioned earlier was not a policy. A written policy should *not* just be a set of aims, goals or targets; a programme of study, a list of needs, a menu of procedures or schemes of work.

So, what are we left with? Caldwell and Spinks (1988) describe it thus:

'A policy is a set of guide-lines which provide a framework for action in achieving some purpose on a substantive issue. The guide-lines specify in general terms the kind of action which will or may be taken... they imply an intention and a pattern for taking action... a framework, often with some basis for discretion, within which the headteacher, staff and others in the school can discharge their responsibilities with a clear direction.

A policy invariably reflects a set of beliefs or values or philosophy on the issue concerned.'

Unpicking this definition, the key words and phrases seem to be:

- '*A framework for action*', implying that the schemes of work, programmes of study will be bolted into this framework but are not the structure itself.

- '*Imply an intention*', this could be interpreted as a lack of clarity or vigour but it provides a link with the overall purpose of the school and its direction.

- '*Invariably reflects a set of beliefs* ...', this is important, for it carries with it the implication that if the school does have a clear set of values and philosophy then these should be reflected in every policy, and takes us towards the notion of having a 'model' policy to which all our policies will conform. More of this a little later.

Moving from what may appear to be a rather abstract description we will stay with Caldwell and Spinks and look at a concrete example of a school policy on 'homework'. This is from a secondary school but will serve the purpose of illustrating the concept.

Regular homework is a valuable aspect of the learning process and contributes to the development of sound study habits.

Consistent with this belief, homework shall be implemented according to the following guide-lines:

1. Each child will be assigned homework in each subject on a regular basis.

2. While the amount of homework will vary according to age and learning needs, every child will be assigned some homework on each day of the school week, with at least two days per week assigned for each of language, maths and social studies.

3. Teachers will be responsible for reviewing the homework assignment for each child.

Shaping the policy

This homework example matches the policy description closely and
exemplifies two other important aspects of policy writing: structure
and conciseness. The policy is in fact quite simply structured and
consists of a rationale or purpose (first paragraph) followed by a set
of three guide-lines. The school is telling the world why it wishes
children to do regular homework and how it's going to be done.

What comes as a surprise to many teachers when they are first
shown this model is the brevity of the statement compared to their
previous experiences of being presented with long documents con-
sisting of several pages and often with additional appendices. These,
as we can now see, were not pure policies but probably included programmes of study and schemes of work for individual year groups.
Conciseness is the target to be aimed for and in fact it is possible to
compose most policy statements on one side of an A4 sheet. However, the structure illustrated here will, in many cases, be too skele-
tal and not satisfy the complexity of many curricula areas and issues
that schools will wish to have policies to cover. We will now look at
an example of policy development which one London school has
been working towards.

The starting point here is the notion of first creating a 'policy for
policies'. Most teachers' reaction to this concept is one of incredu-
lity, and the feeling of creating an extra task just for the sake of some
management theory. In fact it is a sound idea which can lead to many
benefits. Some of these being: a more coherent and rationale
approach across all areas of school life, an opportunity to express the
school's vision and purpose in these areas and the provision of valuable support for teachers inexperienced and, or, lacking in
confidence with policy writing. From a pragmatic point of view,
valuable time and energy may be saved in policy development
through establishing an agreed model to which all policies will conform.

The senior management team and staff of Copenhagen Primary
School in Islington, London, dedicated an INSET day to work
through the idea of writing a 'policy on school policies'. This was
published in draft form for review after a year had elapsed and a trial
run was made using it as the framework for their Physical Education
Policy (see Appendixes II and III for the full version of these documents).

The structure that evolved came under these nine headings:

1. Statement of aims.

2. Equal opportunities.

3. Health and safety (where appropriate).

4. Time and weight in the curriculum.

5. Assessment (including success criteria).

6. Agreed practice (specific baseline expectations).

7. Resources (agreed organisation, roles etc.).

8. Date of staff agreement.

9. Date and procedures for review.

It can be seen that this framework again matches our original model though in greater detail. It has a rationale or purpose, '*statement of aims and equal opportunities*', while the following five headings, 3 to 7, provide a framework for implementation. An interesting addition is the facility to allow for the review of each policy, which carries the implication that the statements are not going to be set in concrete but will allow for change. The confirmation of staff agreement to be attached to each policy also seems a sensible precaution.

This model will enable individual policies to be written to a consistent formula while allowing for flexibility within each document. For instance, this is illustrated in Copenhagen School's PE policy where for obvious reasons there is an extensive paragraph dealing with health and safety issues which, one assumes, would not feature in such detail in other policies. The school is able to express its philosophy and core beliefs under the first two headings and teachers are given quite specific guide-lines for organising and implementing this curriculum area.

A more basic version of this, again from a London school, can be seen in this second model which is seen in a framework for the school's Music Policy:

Policy for music
Rationale:
>   We teach music because ...
Purposes:
>   As a result of teaching music we want to have:
>   1. Children who ...
>   2. Children who ... etc.
Broad guidelines:
>   When teaching music we 1 ...
>   2 ... etc.
Present position:
Future plans:

This much simpler approach could well provide a useful starting point for whole staff discussion around the issue of policy development. Another way forward is to take these models and compare them with the structure and content of existing policies. Could they become more effective if restructured in this way?.

A process model for writing policies

School policies fall, broadly speaking, into two groups.

First, those policies which will generate few disagreements and on which most teachers will have a fairly united view on the issues involved. They might, for instance, include core curriculum areas whose content has been proscribed by the National Curriculum or health and safety where, again legislation will dictate the shape of the school policy. Let us label this group of policies as 'harmonious'.

The second group will be those where disagreement or contention is anticipated, which polarise teachers or which have a high political profile. Hot potatoes. We will, for the sake of this discussion, describe these as 'discordant'. They could include areas such as Sex Education, Control and Discipline or School Uniforms.

The examples given within these two categories must not be taken too literally! One school's discord will be another's harmony. There will be staff groups for whom all policy issues can be dealt without disagreement and others who will battle over every sub-clause in every document.

This leads to the proposition that there needs to be a different approach to policy writing for our two categories of policy. The process is largely similar for both 'harmonious' and 'discordant' but in order to clarify the differences we will look at them separately.

'Harmonious' issues can be dealt with in a straightforward fashion through a process illustrated here:

> **Step 1:** the co-ordinator, or person designated as policy leader, reviews existing practice and collects colleagues' views.
> **Step 2:** the policy is written by the co-ordinator or as a shared task with a small team using an agreed model, i.e.:
> – containing a brief rationale;
> – having a set of guide-lines;
> – using 'plain speak';
> – restricted to one page in length.
> **Step 3:** the draft policy is distributed for consultation.
> **Step 4:** amendments are made to the policy.
> **Step 5:** final version of the policy is published and disseminated throughout school. Staff agreements are recorded and a review date set.

For 'discordant' areas a more considered approach is advisable:

> **Step 1:** a working party is established which represents a range

of interests and expertise. It could, in certain circumstances, be helpful to include governors and/or parents.

Step 2: working party gathers information and views relating to the policy.

Step 3: three policy options are drafted which reflect the perceived spectrum of views.These must conform to a common format.

Step 4: consultation exercise is carried out using the three options to obtain staff consensus.

Step 5: agreed elements are synthesized into a final policy document.

Step 6: final version of policy is published and disseminated throughout the school. Staff agreement recorded and review date set.

As can be seen the process model involving discord is longer and makes more demands on both staff and resources it is however essential, if we take policy development at all seriously, that these areas of contention are dealt with as thoroughly as is possible.

In policy development the involvement of others outside the teaching staff is often worth considering, for example bringing the schoolkeeper or premises manager onto a Health and Safety group would have obvious benefits in terms of practice and knowledge. Schools having pupil representation, maybe in the form of a school council, have brought the children themselves into policy development. This input could be particularly valuable when formulating a policy for playground management or discipline procedures. All policies will have to be presented to Governors at some point and the *Education Reform Act (ERA) 1988* requires governing bodies to review curricula policies. In fact the legislation allows them to go further than this and to draft their own. As a group they will represent a wide range of skills and knowledge and they can be the source of valuable expertise. It may be productive to include a cross section of governors in any consultation exercise being undertaken.

The production of the school's Sex Education Policy is, at the time of writing, the Governors' responsibility though in reality this is usually delegated to headteacher and staff who draft the document for ratification at a governors' meeting.

Summary

The key features for an effective written policy may be summarised thus:

- a written policy is a statement of intent;
- it must be concise – one side of A4 target;

- it should include a rationale and a set of guide-lines;
- its structure should be modelled on the school's 'policy for policies';
- the writing process should reflect the issues – 'harmonious' or 'discordant';
- the process must involve consultation.

As a member of the school's senior management team (SMT) the primary deputy plays a critical and varied role in the field of policy development. These include that of team leader, team member, curriculum specialist, consultant, mentor, and bridge builder.

Managing meetings

The paradox that lies within school management in the 1990s relates to the fact that primary schools are now complex organisations, the original National Curriculum placed impossible demands on classteachers' time and the political stakes that education carries have turned public accountability into public scrutiny. The paradox is that teachers are expected to be doing more, with, apparently, less time in which to do it.

A fundamental process of getting things done in any organisation is the meeting of individuals within the organisation. Naturally we have to get meetings right. The following maxim will provide us with a beacon through the writing that follows:

'Meetings are for getting things done.'

This is not the place to dwell on the possibly universal experience that teachers have of meetings that don't get things done and leave feelings of frustration and of time wasted. Instead we will explore, positively:

- planning and organisation;
- meetings roles;
- a code of practice.

There are aspects of the organisation and running of meetings which are common to a variety of forums. However the deputy's involvement will chiefly come through having to run routine staff-meetings, curriculum development sessions, and smaller team meetings so it is within these contexts that the following ideas and suggestions lie.

Planning and organisation

The organisation of any meeting, whatever its purpose or aims, falls into three distinct phases:

1. pre- meeting;

2. the meeting;

3. post-meeting.

Phase 1: pre-meeting

As in most management processes the success of the meeting will hinge largely on pre-planning. Here is a check-list that needs to be addressed:

1. Purpose: what are the objectives of the meeting? Is it, for example, for communication, consultation or decision making?

2. Involvement: who really needs to be invited? Are all interests going to be represented?

Pause: Does there necessarily have to be a meeting or are there other a ways of dealing with the issues?

3. Notification: all those being invited need to have: date, time, place, and duration, purpose of meeting, agenda with relevant back-up materials, minutes of previous meeting.

4. Venue: is the meeting place appropriate for the kind of meeting being planned? It doesn't always have to be the staff-room. Is the seating adequate and comfortable? Would it be helpful to be seated around a table or not? What kind of refreshments will be appropriate?

5. Preparation: have any materials, handouts, etc., produced well before the meeting date and in sufficient quantities, likewise do your information gathering or reading-up well in advance. Clarify or designate roles for the meeting, i.e. who is to be Chair, minute taker, etc?

6. Immediately prior to meeting: have refreshments prepared, arrange seating as decided and to match, exactly, the numbers expected, have materials at hand and display the agenda prominently.

Phase 2: the meeting

1. Start at the designated time – when this becomes

established practice people will begin to arrive punctually.

2. Clarify roles.

3. Remind group of the meeting's purpose.

4. Confirm finishing time and stick to it – again this must become established practice.

5. Review the agenda and, if necessary, agree a time-slot for each item.

6. Build in time well before the end to review the meeting and confirm decisions made and actions to be taken. This can be done by agreeing the minutes, thus saving time at the next meeting.

7. Arrange next meeting (some staff have found it more useful to do this at the beginning of the meeting).

This is the bare framework for a meeting which will be fleshed out in the sections on roles, guide-lines and a code of practice.

Phase 3: post-meeting

1. Type up and distribute minutes as soon after the meeting as is possible. Establish a system which checks that all parties, including absentees, have received a copy.

2. Communicate decisions made and action to be taken to other relevant people.

3. Publicise time, date, place and purpose of next meeting.

Roles

Meetings can run successfully without having anyone acting in a formal role. Curriculum team, year group or phase meetings are generally conducted informally and frequently without a chairperson. However, experience shows that with larger groups the designation of formal roles is critical in producing outcomes of any value. We will look at roles commonly found in meetings and see what skills, attitudes and procedures are most productive. It is highly recommended that teachers, even before becoming deputies, create the opportunities to practice these roles.

The chair's role

In their professional life, as well as elsewhere, teachers will have observed, and been involved with an extensive range of chairing styles. These will have included exemplars covering the whole leadership continuum from authoritarian to *laissez faire*; from Ghengiz Khan to St. Francis of Assisi. The model being presented here will try to represent the middle road of sensitivity balanced with firmness and commitment.

The chair's prime function is to manage the meeting so that 'things get done'; it is his/her responsibility to ensure that the time is spent in reaching objectives. To some extent this can be achieved through procedures, such as keeping to the agenda, following the steps of introducing each topic, opening up discussion and moving on to decide on action. But the real effectiveness of chairing comes through skills of communicating with, and managing, people. These skills are used to facilitate the processes of the meeting towards achieving its purpose.

Three fundamental processes which happen in meetings are:

- sharing information;

- discussion;

- making decisions.

The chair has to manage these processes so that they are enriched by the whole group's experience and not just those who shout loudest. Their role is that of an orchestral conductor in aiming to achieve a result that is greater than the sum of the individual instruments.

We will now move sequentially through a typical meeting to illustrate these procedures and skills.

1. Opening remarks: These are critical as they set the tone of the meeting. The aims are to:

- Welcome the group.

- Introduce people, as necessary. Give their names, who they represent and their relevance to the meeting.

- State the purpose of the meeting.

- Motivate people at the outset to work towards the purpose. Expand on the main issue. Review previous discussion and emphasise possible benefits and opportunities.

- Run through the agenda, possibly highlighting priorities and allocating time-slots.

These opening remarks will, largely, form the impression that the group will have of the chair. It is well worth preparing them in advance and have them available as written notes.

2. Routine business: The first few items on the agenda are usually routine matters, such as approving previous minutes, noting attendance and taking apologies. They should be dealt with expediently while allowing people to voice disagreement with the accuracy of minutes. People do not like hearing their views recorded incorrectly.

3. Main topic: The chair's tasks are to:

- Introduce the topic. It may be necessary to clarify the parameters of the discussion.

- Invite information, views or presentations from the meeting.

- Encourage discussion.

- Help the group come to a decision.

The challenges in facilitating this process will include:

Remaining impartial: The chair's function is to facilitate the meeting as a whole in reaching its objectives and the outcome may well not accord with his/her views. The temptation should be avoided to exploit the power of the role to influence decisions. There are occasions where a conflict of interest may arise, for example the leadership responsibilities of the deputy may interfere with the chairing role on a particular issue. On such occasions it is advisable to delegate the chairing to another member of the group when, as a participant, the deputy will be free to express their opinions without constraint.

Controlling timing: In order to manage time the chair needs to have a clear plan of the stages to be worked through which should be sketched out in advance. It may help to say something like 'We have ten minutes to discuss the three options before we need to move to a decision.'

Time is often wasted by long-winded or dominant group members. Tactful interruption is the remedy whilst noting that their contribution is valued. Appointing a supportive timekeeper will help here.

Progressing the meeting towards its objective: The chair needs to stand back from the detailed discussion to check where the meeting is going. This means being aware of unproductive processes happening in the meeting, such as:

- The discussion going round in circles.

- Individuals, or the whole group, going off at tangents.

- Personal agendas being pursued.

- Decision making being put off.

Here the chair will need to intervene to refocus the process. The techniques of summarising and using clarifying questioning are effective solutions.

Using active listening and questioning techniques: As well as having an overview of how the meeting is progressing the chair needs to pay close attention to the minutiae of the discussion, This will help in progressing the meeting towards its objective through *active listening* and the *use of questions*:

- *Active listening*: the key skills are reflecting what others have said, particularly if the contribution is unclear, and summarising the points that have been made, before moving the meeting on; skills which teachers use daily in their interaction with children in the classroom.

- *Use of questions*: open questions will help to spur discussion and widen it out. Closed questions are useful in clarifying information and views, focusing the discussion and moving forward. Questions can be addressed to the meeting as a whole, or to individuals if they have a contribution that they are holding back, or for drawing someone into the discussion.

Checking understanding across the group: Individuals may not be aware of the background to particular issues being discussed, or may not fully understand what is being said. If so they will fall behind the group and may be too embarrassed to ask for an explanation. It is the chair's responsibility to identify these moments (watch for puzzled expressions) and to establish the culture where it is 'OK to ask'. It can be helpful to summarise the points made so far and ask whether anyone wants clarification.

Encouraging wide participation: Meetings produce the best outcomes when there is full participation and it is the chair's job to see that this happens. No sleeping partners. The appropriate skills here are *controlling dominant individuals* and *drawing out reticence*.

- *Controlling dominant individuals*: there are often one or two people at a meeting who hold strong views which they wish to expound at every opportunity. This can limit the contribution of others and may call for firm action from the chair. The chair may have to focus on a specific, positive point that has been made by the dominant member and call on others in the group to comment on it. The aim is to avoid alienating the individual while creating space for others. An alternative approach is to ask other individuals for their views first. The adoption by staff of an agreed code of conduct can help in alleviating this problem.

- *Drawing out reticence*: group members may be contributing little through shyness, feelings of not having a role to play, or nursing a grievance. The chair can attempt to overcome these by asking for their contribution on a point where it's known they have a strength, expertise, or knowledge; but not putting the individual on the spot with something they're unsure of and thus diminishing their confidence even further. Feelings of grievance are best explored privately after the meeting.

Managing 'difficult' people: Some people have attitudes and views which are set in concrete and will not be willing to change however cogent the counter arguments that they are exposed to. If they are also dominant group members they can be very effective in blocking or slowing down progress to objectives. It can be energy and time consuming to effect change in these individuals and as the 'meeting' forum is a place for 'getting things done' it may not be appropriate to attempt any transformations during the meeting. Better to move forward by stating that the majority view is clearly different to theirs.

Other difficult personalities that need attention will be those who always end up arguing, either through genuinely held, different views, or through clashes of personality. Arguments need to be interrupted and the meeting's focus shifted onto another aspect of the issue being discussed. Adherence to a code of conduct will certainly help to reduce these problems.

Helping the meeting in making decisions: Once the main topic has been discussed the group will need to make decisions. This can be done in two ways, through consensus or by voting.

Consensus involves discussing a choice of options or proposals until there is widespread agreement on one of them. This can be time consuming, may call upon high-order chairing skills and means ensuring there are no dissenting members whose voice has not been heard.

Voting is more expedient but may sow seeds of grievance from the minority group which may flower at a later date.

Ending the meeting
Aim to tie up the meeting briskly and in a systematic way.

Any other business: The objective here is not to have any 'surprises'. If the agenda was discussed at the beginning of the meeting and if the school has established a system where the agenda is an open one where contributions are welcomed from all then there should be no earth shattering proposals. However the discussion will inevitably open up new avenues and issues which will need to be dealt with. Small matters can be dealt with immediately while more substantial items need to be put on the next agenda. The chair will need to discriminate at this point.

Summarise the meeting: Itemise the progress made, decisions taken and subsequent action needed, individuals designated to take action and any deadlines agreed. This may be done jointly with the 'minute taker'.

Date and time next meeting: This can be a reminder if already fixed at the beginning of the meeting. Establish the habit of diaries being brought along to all meetings.

Thank the meeting: Thank the group for their attendance, emphasising good timekeeping and full participation. Also thank individuals who made presentations or prepared materials.

Effective chairing which facilitates positive and creative outcomes is a rewarding but demanding experience. Chairs will know when it has been done well by the number of people who will give them a quiet and private thanks after the meeting has closed. The skills and techniques to be assimilated are numerous and are only developed through observing effective chairs and experiencing the process oneself. It is recommended that these techniques be practiced in 'safe' situations; in small groups and in the familiar environment of known colleagues before moving into deputy headship where the stakes will be higher and the pressure to 'get it right first time' will be greater.

The role of the minute taker

Many of us will have had this role thrust upon us early in our professional lives without having had any preparation and just picked it up as we have gone along. We will all have also been on the receiving end of the minutes of meetings and we will have observed a huge variety of approaches with wide ranges of detail and accuracy. So is there a definitive model we can examine and is there a standard practice we can apply? The answer to these questions is probably no, and one of the interesting aspects of minute taking is the working through to one's individual style. Having said this there are, of course, basic requirements the minute taker will have to meet and these will be highlighted in looking at the role itself.

But first, who is the minute taker and how do schools allocate this role? What needs to be avoided is an arrangement where the same person takes on the function at every, or the majority of meetings. The exception being when the school delegates the job to the secretary or other non-teaching member of staff. There are two important reasons for this. The first is that the minute taker is, by the nature of the task, largely outside the discussion and is prevented from inputting into the meeting. An individual who habitually becomes minute taker is thus excluded from the school's prime decision-making forum. Of course it has not been unknown for senior management to consciously delegate the role to the 'difficult person' for this very reason! Second, for reasons of professional development it is recommended that the role is rotated through the staff group so giving everyone the opportunity to develop the skills. A simple way of doing this is to organise an alphabetical rota using people's first or surnames.

Guide-lines for the minute taker

Minutes are primarily a record of decisions reached. In formal meetings, once the minutes are signed by the chairperson they are legally binding and may not be altered.

At the start of the meeting the minute taker should ensure they have a copy of the agenda together with any amendments. The first task is to record the time, date and place of the meeting and who is to chair, similarly the finish time should be recorded. Names of people attending need to be reported, at a large meeting it is advisable to circulate an attendance sheet, apologies received by the chair should also be noted.

Minutes should be:

- written up and sent out as soon as possible after the meeting.

Minutes should include:

- a brief description of the problem/item;
- a brief presentation of all the important facts;
- a clear record of decisions made and actions to be taken;
- a note of who is to take action and by what date;
- when appropriate, a summary of the discussion's key points.

An effective way of dealing with the task is to adopt a standard format for all minute takers to use which covers these points. One such model, in the shape of a proforma is offered here and may be adapted as the need arises. It consists of a sheet of A4 divided into columns headed thus:

Agenda item	Summary of main points	Decisions	Action	By whom?	By when?

The role of timekeeper

Meetings of staff in schools are constantly being run beneath the huge swinging pendulum of time constraint. It follows that the time management of meetings, particularly those with a packed agenda, is of critical importance. Many schools have incorporated the role of timekeeper to assist the management of meetings.

The timekeeper will:

- encourage the chair to start on time;

- cue the chair a minute or so before timed agenda items are to finish;

- cue the chair five minutes or so before the agreed finish time.

A code of practice

Discussion with teachers on the subject of meetings will often highlight the fact that negative experiences have not been the result of poor chairing, badly structured agendas or inaccurate minutes, but focus on the behaviour and attitudes of colleagues. The success of any meeting and the quality of its outcomes must largely depend on the approach adopted by individuals in the group. Following such a discussion, during a management training course for primary deputies, a participant produced a copy of her school's code of practice for meetings. It is offered here without comment, not as a proscriptive model, but as a document that others might use as a starting point for discussion at their own school.

Working agreement for staff meetings

As a member of the group I will:

- Listen to what others have to say.

- Respect the views of other people.

- Make positive comments, not 'put downs'.

- When necessary, challenge the statement and not the person.

- Agree to disagree.

- Respect the confidentiality of both the individual and the group.

- Speak for 'me'.

Time management

We have touched several times on time management issues in the contexts of policy writing and meetings management but will now examine the area of the organisation and use of time from a more personal perspective.

Of all the professions, teaching probably provides the most tightly constrained time boundaries. The classteacher's working day is bound by the framework of the timetable. They cannot open their classroom up at 9.10 am when the school day starts at 9 am, the class cannot be taken to assembly at 10 am when in fact it began at 9.50 am, or because the weather is fine they cannot dismiss the class a half an hour before 'home' time. Having said this the parameters set by the timetable do help the organisation and management of the classteacher's time in that much of the day has already been pro-scribed. There are of course, periods outside the confines of the timetable and it is here that many teachers express concern over their management effectiveness.

But we are not just concerned about the classteacher, and need to consider the more complex situation of the deputy as senior man-ager. As has been reflected on earlier it is unlikely that most deputies will not have a class-teaching responsiblity but they are likely to have some release from this task to carry out their wider school man-agement role. It is during these periods that time management will provide the greatest challenge. If these time slots are not used to maximum effect then the deputy will not become an agent of change and development.

What do we know already about the primary deputy's manage-ment of time? The answer is virtually nothing for while there have been numerous studies which have analysed the use of time by head-teachers, deputies have been universally neglected. What studies have shown is that time management is an area which heads have traditionally dealt with poorly. For instance, a fairly consistent stat-istical outcome is that around 70 per cent of headteachers' time is spent in short, unplanned interaction with colleagues, as in the cor-ridor situation of: 'Oh, Sylvia, I know you're on the way to meet the educational psychologist but could I just ask you about my science budget for next year?' It is highly likely that time studies with deputies would record similar results.

Time management is not an exact science. Many solutions in countering time wastage are plain commonsense and focus on care-ful planning for time, which cannot be managed retrospectively and cannot be managed on the hoof. Many strategies found in time man-agement texts first appear simplistic and seem glaringly obvious yet they are often surprisingly effective in practice.

What we will explore during the remainder of this section will be the notion that: first, time management cannot be improved until we discover where time goes, and secondly, though we cannot physically lengthen the school week, strategies can be learned and applied to develop time effectiveness. This will be dealt with by:

- Analysing where time goes.

- Identifying key problems.

- Finding solutions

Analysing where time goes

We can start down the road of self-awareness by conducting a time audit. One mechanism for doing this is to compile a time log. This will be a record of how each day has been spent through an accurate recording of time slots throughout the working period. There are a variety of methods of approaching this, each providing a different set of problems and each having a varying workload attached. The ideal solution would be to have a second person to record the log; a useful study, perhaps for a student teacher?

Figure 3.2 serves as a model for a method which involves the precise recording of each activity during the school day.

Before compiling a log it is helpful to categorise the range of activities that are engaged in during one's professional life. For most teachers the agenda will resemble that shown in Figure 3.1, with each category being allocated a simple coding.

Activities	Code
Teaching	T
Preparation	PR
Assessment and record keeping	RK
Supervision	S
Pastoral care	P
Staff meetings	SM
Team meetings	TM
Parent liaison	PL
Classroom management	CM
Social	S
Peer support	PS
Communication	CM
Curriculum planning	CP

Figure 3.1

The next step is to prepare a log sheet proforma arranged in three columns headed: 'Start time', 'Activity', 'Coding' and 'Duration'.

A day's log, completed by a deputy will serve to clarify this (see Figure 3.2).

Time log – Tuesday			
Start time	Activity	Coding	Duration
8.20	Arrived at school – coffee and chat with cleaner		
8.30	Yr 4 team meeting		
8.45	Head's daily briefing		
8.55	In class prep. maths lesson		
9.10	Saw Rosie's mum re. swimming		
9.15	Class in; register		
9.20	Maths briefing and groupings		
9.30	Class to singing: chaired Jnr staff meeting		
10.00	Maths session		
10.45	Break: playground duty		
11.00	(Non-contact) Set up VCR for Mrs B.		
11.05	Tel. trying to rearrange Jnr. library times		
11.15	Deputised for H/T on Site Man. Committee		
11.32	Sent for by Mrs B – VCR not working		
11.40	Site Man. meeting		
12.00	Snr. Meals Supervisor late, did Inf Dinner Duty		
12.20	Lunch; counselled NQT with discipline problems		
12.30	Chaired Assessment Policy group in H/T's absence		
	etc., etc.		

Figure 3.2

At the end of a long and action packed day the time log is then reviewed.

This next step involves analysing the use of time during the day first by putting each activity into one of the headings already determined, assigning a code letter and noting the duration of the activity. For example:

9.10 am Saw Rosie's mum re. swimming   (Code PL)
(Duration 5m)
and
12.20 pm Lunch; counselled NQT with discipline problems
(Code PS)   (Duration 10m)

The total time spent on each category of activity may then be com-
puted and recorded. Clearly recording just one day's set of activities
will not provide a representative picture of the use of time and the
process needs to be repeated over the period of a week or better still
a fortnight.

At the end of the audit period, either a week or longer, the daily
durations of time are totalled for each category producing a final
result which will resemble the example shown in Figure 3.3. In addition the total times have been converted into percentages of the total
time of the work period.

Activities	Code	Total time	% time
Teaching	T	21hrs	60%
Preparation	PR	5 hrs	14%
Assessment and record keeping etc.	RK	4 hrs	11%

Figure 3.3

There are a few warning notes to be sounded at this point; this
example may not accord with the readers reality, it only represents
time spent in school and ignores time at home, or elsewhere, spent
on preparation and record keeping. A 'teaching total' represented as
60 per cent of total time may not appear at all realistic, but in fact
surveys made of teachers' use of time usually produce a figure of
around 65 per cent.

The result of the time audit now provides a picture of where time
has gone.

Identifying key problems

The analysis can now help us in becoming more effective time managers.

Activities which have a heavy time load can be highlighted
together with some categories to which little time has been given.
This can be illustrated by going back to the deputy whose daily time
log we used earlier.

At the end of a fortnight's audit there were several activities that caused concern by appearing to have occupied disproportionately large chunks of time. These were time totalled for *meetings* and time spent under *peer support*. Each of these need to be examined and the exact nature of the activities identified. Having done this the deputy needed to ask a series of questions. For example when looking at *peer support* these might be: Was the time planned? Was it part of their responsibilities? What were the outcomes, did anyone benefit? Could some of these interactions be delegated elsewhere?

The purpose of this kind of reflection is to identify what is creating the extra load and what kind of solutions might be available to alleviate the time pressure.

When carrying out this self-assessment it is also important to make some kind of estimate of the time you would ideally want to allocate to these activities and to compare this with what the time log has shown. Then consider what obstacles are preventing the achievement of the ideal. This reflection can then move the individual towards identifying specific, concrete steps that may be taken.

Carrying out a personal time audit is not easy, recording it is in itself time consuming, it calls for a systematic approach and a certain amount of doggedness. However, teachers, deputies and heads who have undertaken the task talk of considerable benefits following the exercise which can bring radical changes in their use of time.

Solutions

Having discovered where time goes and identified key problem areas it is up to individuals to find solutions which match their personal situation.

The following is a compendium of ideas, strategies and suggestions, which may help to trigger action. Some of these will be more pertinent to the role of deputy while others may be applied by all teachers.

Avoiding crisis management:

1. Always plan ahead. Keep action dates in your diary which are well in advance of deadline dates. This allows time for unforeseen problems, emergencies and 'Murphy's Law'. Try using a Filofax.

2. Build in thinking time to any project. Don't allow this time to be eroded by other demands.

3. Periodically carry out an audit of how you are using time.

4. Avoid procrastination. Each morning focus on the two or three actions you *least* want to take and tackle them!

Organising paperwork:

1. Establish a workable filing system. Time spent setting one up initially will be recouped manyfold later; ask the school secretary to explain her system.

2. Have a desktop filing system (trays) for short, medium and long-term tasks.

3. Have only the current paper task on your desk at any given time.

4. Display your daily and weekly time plans prominently.

5. When faced with a mountain of paperwork aim to deal with each document *once* only.

   Try using these strategies:
   - *Dumping.* Get rid of the useless or superfluous.
   - *Delaying.* Sort important matters that require careful thought into your 'medium term ' tray.
   - *Delegating.* You will not be the best person to deal with some items. Pass them on to the appropriate colleague.
   - *Doing.* Deal with straightforward issues immediately.

6. Develop the discipline of finishing one task before starting fresh ones.

Action lists:

1. At the end of each day compile a 'Do it!' sheet which lists tasks for the following day. A satisfying ploy is to include an item that has already been done thus starting the next day with something already crossed out.

2. Similarly create a 'Do it' sheet at the end of the week of actions that need to be taken the following Monday. This activity will, in time, become automatic and can provide a valuable system for keeping on top of workloads.

Managing the phone:

1. Arrange to make calls in batches; so that if a number is engaged the time can be used for another call.

2. Use the receiver's 'number recall' facility.

3. A time-saving gambit is to start your conversation with, 'I've only got a couple of minutes so ...'

Interaction with colleagues:

1. When it's appropriate say 'no' without feeling guilty. This may need practicing!

2. Set time for meetings with colleagues; avoid responding to the 'Can I have a quick word' approach in the corridor.

3. Agree the length of time to be spent when discussing an issue with a colleague.

4. Closing your door when engaged in a task will help to reduce time lost through interruptions. Suggest the adoption of a code of practice for staff to reduce unnecessary interruptions.

Meetings:

1. Follow the time management ideas previously outlined.

Problem solving:

1. Adopt systematic approaches.

The three major management areas dealt with in this chapter are not exclusive to the role of the primary deputy, for the skills, strategies and approaches which help make them effective are essential to all teachers. They have been included in Part I of this book, 'Preparation for ...', as techniques and skills which can be acquired by classteachers approaching the move to senior management.

Part II
Induction

4 Becoming a senior manager

Moving into a new professional role can be an exciting and demanding experience but for the unwary the path may be littered with unexposed hazards. The underlying strategies for managing this change must involve forward planning and include information gathering and awareness raising. So that even before the first day of taking up their post the newly appointed deputy will have done a considerable amount of preparation.

This chapter will look at aspects of the early stages of deputy headship, namely:

- Before the event.

- Taking the plunge.

- Relationships with colleagues.

- Head and deputy: leadership, structure and responsibilities.

- Reviewing the job description

Before the event – putting the pieces together

The school

The well organised teacher will have gathered a degree of data about the school during the initial stages of applying for the deputy headship. Having been offered the job they should seek access to the documents, policies and reports which will provide an intimate portrait of the school's internal systems and methods of working. A reading list for the period left before taking up the post could usefully includes;

- A list of all staff, both teaching and non-teaching, with their roles and responsibilities.
- All written policies including those still in draft form.
- Current and previous year's budget statements.
- The current and previous School Development Plan (SDP).
- Copies of any recent inspection reports.
- Details of recent INSET and staff development activities.
- Copy of the governors' annual report.
- List of governors together with any special responsibilities/ interests.
- Minutes (non-confidential) of the last couple of governors meetings.
- Staff meeting minutes.
- School brochure or handbook plus other documents sent to parents.
- Parents' newsletter file.
- Minutes of PTA meetings.

These will only be available, for obvious reasons, with the head's agreement. But there will clearly be enormous advantages from both sides that they are provided. A useful strategy to deal with what could be a considerable pile of documentation is to plan a series of meetings together to discuss and clarify the reading that the deputy designate will have done. For convenience these could be arranged to cover specific areas such as 'Governors', 'Organisation and planning', 'Parents', etc. Involvement of others, such as the chair of governors, would further enhance the value of these discussions as well as provide personal contact with key members of the school's community.

The LEA

For those teachers coming from a different LEA there will be another range of data that needs to be gathered: about the local authority. Most of this can be found at the new school but a more interesting and worthwhile move is to arrange to meet the school's Inspector at the Education Office and ask to be introduced to key personalities. Useful names, and contact numbers to have would includes;

- the Education Officer or Director of Education;
- the Chief Inspector;
- individual specialist Inspectors;
- Education Welfare Officer;
- Educational Psychologist;
- Buildings Officer or Architect.

The Teachers' Centre

Another source of support and information that may be usefully tapped is the local Teachers' Centre, or Professional Development Centre, this is particularly important when the deputy designate is 'out' borough. Personal contact with the Centre leader and staff will pay dividends later and a picture of the resources and support available will help in the very likely event that the deputy will be taking on responsibility for staff development. The Centre will often be found to be the home of any advisory teachers still retained by the local authority and discussing the support they can provide will be valuable. Many areas have established Primary Deputies' Support Groups and the Centre will be the place to find details of their programme and contact numbers.

Names and faces

It is not unheard of for newly appointed deputies to leave it until the first day of term before being introduced to colleagues, children and parents. This is an approach that is not very helpful, though in very rare situations, perhaps due to geography, cannot be avoided. It is recommended that during the half-term, or longer, before the official starting day, there is a gradual integration into the school by the new deputy, through a series of visits and involvement.

It may be necessary for the deputy designate to take the initiative and make it their business to get invited to as many events as possible at their future school. These might include;

- observing a Governors' meeting;
- attending forward planning staff meetings;
- attending parent-run social events;
- attending children' s sports, shows, concerts, etc.

A word of caution may be necessary at this point. Although others will certainly be making their private assessments of the deputy it will not be appropriate for these occasions to be used to start establishing their authority and certainly not to be making judgements or expressing criticism of any kind. It would be advisable to clarify these issues with the Head before the events take place. In addition useful time may be spent with the outgoing deputy and senior members of staff who are perhaps part of the senior management team.

Taking the plunge

The advantages of having carried out the information gathering and general getting to know who's who suggested above will be shown immediately the new term starts. The deputy will not be floundering to remember names and roles and will be able to become involved in staff meeting discussions from an informed and confident stand-point. The initial honeymoon period that most newcomers are granted will, however, not be lengthy. The process that they will have experienced previously on taking over a new class when children test the boundaries of acceptable behaviour, will be mirrored by co-workers, parents and pupils in their new role.

During the first few weeks of appointment there will be key events and actions that will need to be organised and implemented to near perfection as they will form the basis on which others will make their assessments and judgements. They could include the following.

First assembly   This will be the most public of all events and will require careful preparation. Note will need to have been made about the established routines that the children are accustomed to; the coming in, the going out, the sitting, the standing. It is recommended that these patterns are kept to initially. The main objective at this first assembly is to make an impact. To demonstrate to the staff that the children can be controlled, that their attention can be won and that the deputy has something interesting and lively to communicate. The content of the assembly must be constructed around these issues. It won't be right first time but it should be quite close to right. New deputies who haven't had much opportunity to take assemblies in the past will need to talk through their planning with the head and perhaps take a look at one or two of the numerous texts dealing with the primary assembly.

First staff meeting   It is extremely likely that the running of a staff meeting will be delegated to the deputy during the early stages of their appointment. What needs to be avoided is having the first meeting dumped on them unexpectedly by the head without the chance to plan the process. The chairing of this meeting can be stressful as the deputy will, perhaps for the first time, be under the magnifying glass of the staff group. The solution, of course, lies in thorough preparation and planning. If the procedures discussed in Chapter 2 are followed then the meeting should progress well and, for colleagues whose previous experience of staff meetings has not been a positive one, could provide an eye-opener which will certainly enhance the credibility of the deputy.

Deputizing for the head   Sooner rather than later the newly appointed deputy will be called upon to deputize for an absent head-teacher. This absence from the premises will be a planned or an unplanned event each calling for different strategies to manage the situation.

When the Head knows that they will be away for a definite period of time, perhaps at a conference or attending a course then the situation that the deputy will be faced with will be quite straight-forward. The head's diary will have been cleared, ensuring few visitors, and a predetermined return date means that much decision making can be deferred until that time. What can create a greater management problem is the unexpected absence of the head due to illness or other emergencies. The deputy will have to decide whether to cancel meetings, assemblies, visitors and a host of other tasks the head has planned. As a general rule, and especially when the deputy has a classteaching responsibility, the first move is to go through the head's diary with the secretary and postpone all non-urgent tasks. This will reduce to a manageable level the extra workload that has to be taken on. The second strategy would be for the deputy to look at their own commitments to identify tasks that may be delegated on to others. Finding a supply teacher, budget allowing, is an obvious early move if the absence looks like being prolonged.

Many new deputies find this first opportunity to step into the Head's shoes, even for a short period of time, a testing experience. It might also be said that others will use the opportunity to test the deputy. The following suggestions may help those facing the situation:

- inform the chair of governors and Local Education Office of head's absence (though not for short periods of time);

- when in doubt consult the above;

- temporarily reduce own commitments to a minimum;

- without appearing indecisive, defer important decision making until the head's return;

- whenever possible maintain regular contact with the head;

- try to keep routines going, such as assemblies, staff meetings, etc.;

- establish a high profile around the school, i.e. playtimes, dinnertimes, start and end of the day;

- don't allow any slipping in the organisation of the day, i.e. unofficial extensions to playtime, classes being allowed out earlier than scheduled, etc;

- keep teaching and non-teaching staff informed about the situation and the actions you are taking;

- keep a diary of the period to provide a basis for useful discussion on the head's return.

Relationships with colleagues

An aspect of the settling in period which may cause anxiety for some is the establishment of the deputy/colleagues relationship. The nature of the change from classteacher is radical and probably represents the largest shift in perspective that a teacher will make in their professional life; greater for instance than the move from deputy to headship. For internally appointed deputies the issues that need to be dealt with may be even more acute.

What then are the implications and consequences of the change, the metamorphosis, from classteacher to senior manager ?

We have already touched upon this earlier when it was suggested that the consequences of the changed relationship with teaching colleagues might cause some people to pause and reconsider the move to management in the first place.

The core, and inescapable fact, is that the deputy has opened, and gone through, the gate of management and that things are fundamentally different on the other side. They are going to be paid more to accept greater responsibility, which includes having to manage people and systems within the school. However egalitarian the management ethos is and whatever the extent of consultation and collaborative working, they will have become part of the powers that be; 'a chief' rather than an 'Indian' and in some situations, 'one of them'.

From the first days in post the deputy will have to establish clear understandings with colleagues of how their relationship with them will operate, the boundaries of confidentiality they wish to set and how they will deal with the inevitable moans and groans about senior management. The guide-lines that follow have been compiled through discussion with numerous new deputies and will be worth considering by those struggling to lay the foundations of a healthy professional relationship.

- As a senior manager your prime responsibly and loyalty belongs to the SMT.

- Refuse to align with any one faction within the staff, however right their cause may appear.

- Avoid involvement in staffroom discussion which criticises the head or other individuals in their absence.

- Arrange to listen to gripes in privacy.

- Before receiving confidences make it clear that if the disclosure has an effect on the functioning of the school then the information may have to be passed on to the head.

- Avoid the quick chat in the corridor; specify times to see people.

- Pin this notice up in front of your desk: 'I will not become a "go-between" or a "go-for" '.

The potential pressure created by the demands of colleagues, both teaching and non-teaching on the deputy cannot be over emphasised. As they become more established and develop the trust and confidence of the staff the greater will be these demands. Interpersonal aspects, whether counselling, advising or providing a professional shoulder should not be allowed to erode the prime function of management. To monitor this aspect of the role a periodic analysis, using time logging described earlier, is recommended to provide an objective picture of the use of time

Head and deputy: the team

Much time and energy during this early period of deputy headship must be dedicated to the establishment of what lies at the heart of the effective school: the working and personal relationship that develops between the two key figures in the school, the head and deputy. The critical importance that is attached to the success of this relationship has been highlighted in studies made to identify what are the fundamental aspects of school effectiveness.

One of these pieces of research was a substantial study made of a group of London junior schools carried out over five years in the mid 1980s, by a team led by Peter Mortimer (Mortimer, Sammons, Stoll, Lewis and Ecob, 1988).

The research identified 12 key factors, measures of effectiveness, which make schools places where children make progress. This is what was written about the second key factor:

> 'The involvement of the deputy head.
>
> Our findings indicate that the deputy head can have a major role to play in promoting the effectiveness of junior schools. where the deputy was frequently absent, or absent for a prolonged period ... this was detrimental to pupils' progress and development. Moreover a change of deputy tended to have negative effects. The responsibilities undertaken by deputy heads also seemed to be significant. Where the head generally involved the deputy in policy decisions, it was beneficial to the pupils. This was particularly true in terms of allocating teachers to classes. Thus, it appears that a certain amount of delegation by the headteacher, and the sharing of responsibilities, promoted effectiveness.'

A key phrase here is *the sharing of responsibilities*, for this will provide us with a theme for our examination of the development of the senior team.

Research, particularly of an empirical nature, around the role of the deputy has never been extensive and the professional relationship between head and deputy rarely examined. However, one study which provides an insight into this often fragile liaison is provided in 'One Finger One Thumb' by Jennifer Nias (*Readings In Primary School Management*: Ed Southworth, 1989). The writing, which was the outcome of a piece of action research in the school involved, describes in close detail the delicate relationship which had been established between head and deputy and how this was maintained in spite of a number of threats and tensions. It is recommended reading for the new, or soon to be appointed, deputy.

Factors influencing the working of the SMT

The nature of the working relationship between the two most senior members of staff will be determined by three major influences, namely:

- style of leadership;

- management structure;

- division of responsibilities.

Numerous other factors will, of course, enter the equation. These might include the 'chemistry' between the pair, the introvert/extrovert balance, gender issues, and interpersonal aspects that transactional analysis demonstrates affect all our work relationships. These, however, come outside the ambit of our discussion and we will focus in turn on the three management areas listed above.

Style of leadership

Leadership and management styles are interdependent and although what is written here will refer specifically to leadership the ideas and information are transferable to styles of management.

The new deputy will be joining a team led by the headteacher who will, in most cases, have developed a personal leadership style and who will have his/her own ideas about the leadership required by the job. The deputy will, through past teaching experience, have observed a range of leadership styles and will realise that there is no 'one way' of providing leadership. Texts written on leadership theory abound and those interested in exploring this area of management more thoroughly will find a suggested reading list at the end of the book. In order to clarify what we mean by leadership style it will be helpful at this point to describe briefly what current thinking tells us about leadership in schools. Early ideas held that leadership was a function of personality and personal characteristics; the image of the 'charismatic' leader springs to mind. This picture of certain individuals possessing timeless leadership qualities is, however, not borne out by close examination although we will all have met people, possibly headteachers, who lead through personality alone. Studies of leadership arrived at the conclusion that effective leadership had something to do with *leadership style* which in turn related to the context of the organisation being led. During the 1930s and 40s there evolved a concept of leadership which suggested that an individual's leadership style lay somewhere along an axis which stretched from *authoritarian* at one extreme to *laisez faire* at the other, with *democratic* sitting comfortably in the middle.

Authoritarian————*Democractic*————*Laissez faire*

Naturally in this model the desired style to be achieved by the leader lay within the democratic slot.

Later research into leadership identified two key dimensions: *personal relationships* and *task achievement*. In other words the effective leader ensures that tasks are done while, at the same time, enabling colleagues to feel valued and recognised. The task-orientated leader will be primarily concerned about achieving results whilst the people orientated leader's first concern will be for fostering good relationships. Of course, few of us would see ourselves as having a bias totally to one or the other; most leaders are concerned about both dimensions. Supporters of this theory believe that the extent to which we lean towards one concern or the other determines our dominant leadership style. This concept may be illustrated in a graphical form on the grid shown in Figure 4.1 by registering 'people concern' along a 'Y' axis and 'task concern' along the 'X' axis. Where the co-ordinates meet lies the area which describes one's personal leadership style.

Solicitous
Thoughtful attention to needs of people for satisfying relationship leading to a comfortable, friendly organisation atmosphere and work tempo.

Motivational/problem solving Work achieved by committed people; interdependence through common stake in organisation's purpose leads to mutual trust and respect

Administrative
Adequate organisation performance is possible through balancing need to achieve results whilst maintaining peoples morale

Passive political
exertion of minimum effort to get enough work done to sustain membership of organisation

Aggressive
Prime purpose to achieve results. Work conditions arranged to ensure minimum interference from human factors.

X ....>

Figure 4.1 Leadership style grid

Having an awareness of one's individual approach will be useful in the early stages of the developing relationship with the head. It may help to explain and overcome difficulties that have arisen and it may enable the team to share responsibilities and duties more efficiently through exploiting the leadership strengths of each partner.

The management structure
The second factor likely to have a strong bearing on the functioning of the senior team is how the head perceives the way in which the team will operate. While this will largely be shaped by the leadership and management style of the head, and so in most cases the incoming deputy will be slotting into an established structure, this could be the time to review existing practice with the possibility of introducing change.

Traditionally the management of primary schools has been seen as a straightforward system of top-down, hierarchical management, perhaps looking something like Figure 4.2.

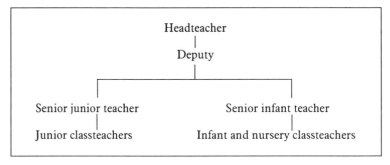

Figure 4.2

In this model, which may well be the only one the new deputy will have experienced, there are a number of advantages. But, within the context of intercommunicating roles and responsibilities and the requirement to deliver, and be accountable for intricate programmes of study there are large disadvantages. Life isn't that simple any more.

Some benefits of structuring the management of the school in this way are clearly apparent. There is likely to be a sense of order with a clear line management structure visible to the whole school community. Delegation may be done simply by passing tasks down the ladder and each member of staff will have a clear idea of their line manager. It can also provide an impression of continuity and stability to the wider school community of parents and governors; they will feel they know 'who's who and who's doing what'. The drawbacks of this model centre to a certain extent around the number of responsibilities that the primary school of the 1990s has to cover and the difficulty of incorporating these within a hierarchical structure. Another difficulty is the limiting effect it can have on individual teacher's professional development and the risk of teachers developing too narrow a view of their role within the school. But even if we ignore these negative factors the hierarchical model has been condemned from all sides through research made into what makes school management effective . The critical factor that this system excludes is simply the involvement of all teachers. They are not brought fully enough into planning and decision making and the mechanism doesn't allow for adequate consultation or collaboration.

If we return to *School Matters*, this is what was written in relation to the involvement of teachers, again one of the study's 12 key factors for school effectiveness:

> In successful schools, the teachers were involved in curriculum planning and played a major role in developing their own curriculum guide-lines. As with the deputy head, teacher involvement in decisions concerning which classes they were to teach was important. Similarly we found that consultation with teachers about decisions on spending was associated with greater effectiveness. It appears that schools in which teachers were consulted on issues affecting school policy, as well as those affecting them directly, are more likely to be successful. We found a link between schools where the deputy was involved in policy decisions and schools where teachers were involved. Thus, effective schools did not operate a small management team – everyone had their say.

'Everyone had their say'. To many deputies this could sound like a recipe for chaos and a prime excuse for not getting things done. So, if we believe that consultation and collaboration with whole staff involvement is the way forward to more effective management, what alternative is there to the hierarchical model?

Collegiality
One option is the notion of *collegiality*.

A collegial structure is one which flattens the pyramid of hierarchy and turns it into a 'solar system' with, at the centre, a managing group led, or chaired, by the headteacher around which orbits a number of satellites, each of which has separate tasks and responsibilities. The central group whose prime function is to make decisions and to have an overall management view of the organisation could, in a small school, include the whole staff or at the other extreme be composed only of the SMT.

Each 'orbiting body' is given sole responsibility for a particular aspect of the organisation and has agreed parameters for independent decision making, resourcing and budgeting. It will have a key person designated to lead the team, usually the person with the greatest knowledge or expertise in the particular area

For the success of this approach to school management there must be clear, unambiguous, communication routes set up and regular reporting back to the centre.

Many primary schools will in fact have moved towards collegiality, without giving it the label, through the setting up of curriculum teams for specific subjects under the leadership of a curriculum co-ordinator. These teams will often operate in the way described above and schools would find the shift to full collegiality simply a matter of increasing the number of satellites to embrace non-curricula areas such as 'record keeping and assessment', 'parent liaison', etc. The composition of each orbiting team need not be restricted to teaching staff but may be enriched by the inclusion of parents, governors and non-teaching staff.

Collegiality is an effective way of managing the School Development Plan which often incorporates several projects and priorities which need central monitoring and evaluation. Positive aspects of this approach include: the development of the autonomy of class teachers, the sharing of the management load across the school with a corresponding lifitng of pressure from the head and deputy and the sharing of individuals' aptitudes and specialist knowledge.

It would be unwise, of course, for incoming deputies to start by demanding for change in existing, perhaps long-established management practices but they will need an awareness that the traditional management pyramid can be tilted a little.

Division of responsibilities
The third, and final, aspect which will have a bearing on the working relationship between head and deputy is the sharing of management responsibilities; the carving of the management cake.

As a starting point it will be useful to identify what these responsibilities might be. Individual schools will produce differing menus, but Figure 4.3 is a composite list of tasks and responsibilities produced by a group of deputies during a management training course.

- team-work with H/T (SMT);
- deputising for H/T;
- teacher appraisal;
- budgeting;
- School Development Planning;
- organising INSET;
- timetabling;
- liaison with HE institutions;
- taking assemblies;
- interview planning;
- implementing and monitoring policies.
- liaison with staff, parents and governors;
- accepting delegated tasks;
- resource management;
- acting as a staff/head filter;
- teaching: being an exemplar/role model;
- support and understanding colleagues;
- observing governors' meetings;
- maintaining school ethos;
- organising suply cover;
- monitoring attendance/ punctuality;
- tidying staffroom.

Figure 4.3

Readers will be able to add their own dishes to the menu and already in this book we have touched upon many other aspects of the role.

A way forward in sorting out the division of responsibilities is for head and deputy to dedicate time, as soon as is feasible after taking up the post, to brain-storm all the management tasks that exist and are likely to arise in the future. The result, which will look similar to the list above, then needs to be grouped into categories. The most useful way of doing this is under headings such as *curriculum, administration, organisation, pastoral care*, etc. This exercise will create some kind of order out of apparent chaos and more importantly lead to reflection and discussion of each issue and thus begin to develop a consensus between head and deputy on what the management priorities are for the school.

The next stage in this process is to list the skills, expertise and knowledge held by each and to begin to match these, as appropriate, to the need and priorities that have been highlighted. This discussion and process might well include other, senior members of staff who are seen as part of the SMT.

Such a review of the management requirements of the school can be fruitful when carried out periodically and certainly whenever there is a change in senior management. It will certainly lead to changes in the role of the deputy and could mean a review of the existing job description.

Job description review
It may appear to be a curious notion to think about reviewing the deputy's job description (JD) at this point so soon after the deputy's appointment but there are a number of possible benefits in so doing. The appointment will have been made probably using the previous post holders JD and undoubtedly the successful candidate will have been able to match its requirements. However, there are likely to be strengths, expertise and talents held by the new deputy which are not matched in the existing document. Another aspect could be the desire of the head and deputy to shift, or change the menu of management responsibilities he/she and the deputy will share. A third influence is likely to be the changing wider educational context and the need for the school to take on board new or modified responsibilities resulting from legislation or LEA policies.

The process for undertaking the review would be the model for managing change first seen in chapter one and shown in Figure 4.4

In this case the *audit* would be examining each clause in the existing JD and then through prioritising deciding what to exclude, retain or change. At the same time the strengths of the new deputy need to be considered. The changing needs of the school organisa-

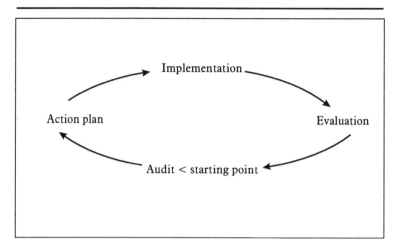

Figure 4.4 Management of change cycle

tion and its management will also provide food for thought at this stage. The *action plan* would include agreeing the format of the revised document its drafting and production. It would be also advisable at this juncture to bring in other members of the SMT and to consult them over the proposed changes. A date could be set at this stage for an evaluation of the job description, say in a year's time. *Implementation* could be as soon as the final version has been agreed. It is important that the whole of the staff are made aware of changes in the deputy's role and politic that the chair of governors also be informed. Periodic *evaluation* of all job descriptions, not only of the deputy but of all staff, is a healthy and necessary routine to incorporate into the cycle.

The framework of a mdoel job description for a primary deputy will be found in Appendix IV.

5 School communication

During the early period of deputy headship there will be a number of aspects of school management that will be have to be tackled and learnt in a short period of time. Some of these issues will previously have been of little concern to the class teacher while others may have been experienced through observation and working with senior members of staff. The next few chapters will explore the background of some of these areas which deputies will be able to apply to their own situations.

We will start by looking into the potentially problematic area of school communication. But why spend time on this subject? Communication, or rather the lack of it, causes problems. Probably the most widespread complaint of those working in any organisation is that 'Communications are terrible!' The reader will only have to think back over the last few days, or week, at school to remember hearing remarks such as; 'I'm always the last to hear', or "The nursery staff never get notified' and 'Well my class didn't get the letter until after home-time' etc.

Good communication lies at the heart of the effective school for however well planned and formulated the policies, systems and organisation, they will never lift off without the wings of communication.

Breaking down the subject we will now examine:

- Communication in organisations.
- The purpose of school communication.
- Internal and external systems.
- Trouble shooting.

Communication in organisations

It will be helpful initially to pull away from the intimate microcosm of the staffroom and the seemingly constant complaints about lack of communication and to take a look at the wider world. Schools, of course, are very special places with their own, sometimes idiosyncratic, ways of organising themselves, nevertheless they do share many aspects of organisation of other institutions, for instance hospitals, banks, supermarkets, or a large office. All organisations share a need to communicate; to communicate within the organisation and to communicate with the outside world.

There has been a considerable amount of research and study made of organisational communication on which we in schools might profitably reflect. Here is a summary of the kind of conclusions that these studies have reached:

The first idea we find is that communication within any organisation is based on four fundamental concepts;

1. Communication is perception.

2. Communication is expectation.

3. Communication makes demands.

4. Communication and information are different and largely opposite – yet interdependent.

1. *Communication is perception.* What this means is that it is the recipient perceiving the communication who makes communication possible; unless there is someone at the other end to hear there will be no communication. The communicator makes it possible, or impossible, for the recipient to perceive.

   We can only perceive what we are capable of perceiving; for most of us a language such as Danish or Swahili is outside our perception so we cannot receive communication in those languages. In other words communication has to be made in terms of people's experience; using a common language.

2. *Communication is expectation.* We perceive what we anticipate perceiving; we see, largely, what we expect to see. The unexpected is often misunderstood or not received at all. So, before we can communicate effectively we must be aware of what the recipient wants to see or hear.

3. *Communication makes demands.* Communication is propaganda. The sender of communication wants to get something across. Demands are being made; for the recipient to do something, believe something or change in some way.

4. *Communication and information are different and largely opposite – yet interdependent.* The difference between the two is that communication is all about perception and information is based on logic. Communication may be informal and personal whereas information is generally formal and impersonal. Their interdependence lies in the fact that the dissemination of information depends on the pre-establishment of communication.

When considering communication within their school these ideas and concepts can provide a useful launching point for the deputy and staff and may well provide pointers in identifying strengths and weaknesses within the systems and customs established in the school. A practical starting point for an SMT or whole staff might be to take these headings and relate them to their local situation and to identify how the school's current practice matches the ideas they represent.

The purpose of school communication

Whenever one sets about examining an area of school management, perhaps with the aim of improving practice or in the pursuit of solutions to problems, a productive starting point is to analyse the purpose of the particular management activity. So in looking at school communication we need to sort out what are its purposes. Brainstorming the question, 'What are the purposes of communication in school?', with groups of teachers will produce a fairly consistent list with which most of us would find little to dispute. The agenda would include items such as:

- 'inform the outside world what we're doing.'

- 'helps cement people together.'

- 'aids consistency across school.'

- 'keeps us on the right track.'
- 'helps with problem solving.'
- 'lessens misunderstandings.'
- 'saves time.'

Once a group of people within an organisation begin to make this kind of analysis of purposes it is much easier to then go on to look at what is happening in reality and whether the communication systems being operated are actually furthering these aims. This brainstorming exercise could be incorporated as part of a 'trouble shooting' task when there are perceived difficulties with communication in the school. More of this a little later. Returning briefly to the wider context of organisational communication research we find that there are *Four purposes for communication* (see Figure 5.1).

Communication for sharing the compelling vision	Communication for integrating the effort
Communication for making intelligent decisions	Communication for sustaining a healthy community

Figure 5.1

Comparing these purposes with the outcomes of our brain-storm it can be seen quite clearly that each of the items fits into one or other of these categories, for example 'Aids consistency across school' matches 'Communication for integrating the effort' and 'Helps with problem solving' comes under 'Communication for making intelligent decisions'.

Again, this matrix can provide a useful focus for staff discussion around communication and may help to depersonalise contentious issues by providing a wider context for the debate.

Internal and external communication

The fundamental, and rather obvious, difference in these two communication systems lies in the fact that the recipients of each will have differing needs, priorities and perceptions. The prime audience for external communication will be the children's parents and the principal form of communication will be written. Schools need to communicate with parents for a number of different purposes; to inform, to request their help and support or to illicit their opinions and views being among the most common. Many schools have found that an effective way of doing this is through sending parents a regular newsletter which contains a mixed menu of straight information, pleas for help with specific events and reports of children's activities. This, if composed in a user-friendly style, can be an effective way to convey what the school wants parents to know.

The two guiding principles for this method of communicating with the outside world are clarity and consistency. Without being patronising the style in which the newsletter is written must ensure maximum accessibility for the parents; the school must speak in a common language. It must also, of course, at the same time make every effort to cater for groups within the school's parent community whose language is other than English.

The writing skills demanded by the person or persons delegated to produce the newsletter are not inconsiderable. In the pursuit of clarity and readability jargon and 'education speak' must be avoided at all costs and an informal conversational style be aimed for. The task of producing the document usually falls onto the head. Schools need to reflect whether this is always the most appropriate person and whether a collaborative effort might not be more effective; involvement of the deputy would certainly be advisable.

Consistency means not only keeping to a familiar look and writing style for each newsletter but also keeping to agreed production deadlines; often a difficult commitment to fulfil particularly for heads. The frequency of production of a parents' newsletter seems to vary considerably from, at one extreme, termly to once a week at the other. Experience appears to show that the more frequent its appearance the more impact there is and the greater is the response of parents to its contents. Individual schools have to weigh up carefully the benefits of frequent production against the cost in terms of time and other resources.

The effective school will have in place internal systems and practices aimed to enable both written and spoken forms of communication to be used with *clarity, conciseness* and *avoiding ambiguity*. To promote this a set of guide-lines can help staff in maintaining a consistent approach to internal communication.

The following mixed bag of suggestions contains nothing startlingly new but includes tried and tested strategies, ideas and systems which have been found to support and facilitate these aims and they could be usefully incorporated into a communication policy or guide-lines.

- **Senior management team:**
  - early morning briefing, review of the day;

- pre-staff meeting briefing;
- Friday lunch: review the week, preview week to come.

- **Whole staff:**
  - short pre-school briefing;
  - planned programme of meetings dates set well in advance;
  - all meetings structured and to follow agreed guide-lines (see Meetings Chapter 3);
  - regular meetings of SMT and non-teaching staff.

- **Staffroom display:**
  - weekly programme of activities;
  - daily news-sheet or day-book – staff required to sign as seen and free to add comments;
  - agenda suggestions sheet for staff meetings;
  - latest, and past s/meeting minutes;
  - minutes (non-confidential) of governors' meetings;
  - an area reserved for INSET information.

- **In-tray/out-tray:**
  - clear procedures for distribution of mail and incoming literature together with a named person with this responsibility;
  - fail-safe systems to ensure two-way flow of confidential information between school and outside agencies (social services, LEA, Education Welfare, etc.).

Trouble shooting: communication breakdown

As has been inferred throughout this chapter school communication is rarely looked at until problems, or what are perceived as problems occur. It is one of those aspects of school management where generally speaking an 'If it ain't broke don't fix it' approach is taken. Given the tight constraints on people's time and resources this is an understandable and seemingly rational attitude. However no communication procedures can ever be perfect and even where few critical problems have arisen it is recommended that a periodic review of the systems and practice in place be undertaken.

The newly appointed deputy will be well placed to lead a review of this kind. The advantages of their taking this on would be that they are bringing a fresh eye to bear on the existing systems, have no vested interest in maintaining ineffective practice and the review process itself will enhance and deepen their knowledge of the organisation and the networks, both overt and covert, operating within it.

The approach being suggested here will have two components:

- Data gathering.
- Communication routes mapping.

Data gathering   The purpose here is to gather the views of as many groups and individuals who are caught up in, and perhaps also those who are excluded from, the school's communication networks. These networks will, of course, involve both internal and external systems so data collection would include gathering information from across a range of parents and governors as well as staff within the organisation.

The most straightforward approach is to compile a questionnaire which is designed to focus on particular issues or which is of a more general nature. The format of the questionnaire should include scope for the recipients to be able to express their views and make suggestions as well as making simple tick-box responses.

On completion the responses will need careful evaluation and analysis and a summary written of the survey's outcomes. This quick snapshot of communication through the school has provided a revealing and constructive way forward for those heads and deputies who have tried the exercise, and has enabled them to incorporate new ideas and drop inefficient strategies which might otherwise have chugged along unnoticed.

Communication routes mapping   Routes mapping invol-ves producing a graphical representation of the communication networks and systems in the school which highlights individuals and groups who are touched by the networking. It can be done with a focus on internal communication or may target external communication or can be a combination of the two. The outcome of the task should help identify what is working well, highlight areas for development and show where individuals fit into, or are excluded from, the system.

The process, step by step, is as follows:

1. Consider how communication happens in the school, the formal and informal pathways and networks – the previous sections will have provided plenty of food for thought.

2. Conjure up an image of the school as some kind of physical object (doing this exercise with groups of teachers produces some startling images such as rainbows, trees, umbrellas, solar systems and even icebergs!).

3. Draft the image onto a sheet of A4 paper as a schematic model and place individuals and groups, as appropriate, on the drawing.

4. Transfer the draft onto a sheet of A1 or A2 paper.

5. Using different coloured felt tip pens superimpose the communication routes you have identified at the first step onto the large drawing.

The resulting tangle of lines should provide a picture of who are the key figures in the networks and perhaps where the systems are failing to reach certain parts of the organisation. The diagram can also be used as an effective and powerful tool for a staff workshop or review of school communication and in conjunction with the outcome of data collection may lead to informed changes in practice.

It can be a fascinating and entertaining process which can be carried out by an individual deputy or, better still, in tandem with the head or in fact any other member of staff each comparing their outcomes at the end of exercise.

6 Team-work

The likelihood is that the newly appointed deputy will have had some experience as a classteacher of working within teams whether as a member of a curriculum team, year group team, School Development Planning team and, as a curriculum co-ordinator, they may even have taken on the role of team leader. There is an equally strong likelihood that they will have been drafted into these team situations with little preparation and a low awareness of how teams work. The purpose of this chapter is to fill these gaps in understanding and to help prepare deputies to become more effective team members and leaders.

As a senior manager, from time to time, the deputy will be required to undertake specific tasks in relation to teamwork. These could include: setting up a team, designating team membership, team building and team leadership at the same time being an active member of the SMT. What follows has been structured to provide some ideas, strategies and, hopefully, a little insight aimed to match these different aspects of teamwork.

The areas to be spotlighted will be:

- Why a team?

- Team roles.

- Team building.
- Leading the team.

Why a team?

At the outset it will be useful for the deputy to have some ideas
sorted out about the purpose of teamwork. Why set up a team when
perhaps the project or task to accomplished could, seemingly equally
well, be taken on by an individual? This question will be asked by
some colleagues who, perhaps, in the past have had negative experiences of team work and are resistant to their further involvement.

Let us kick off with a simple definition of a team. Within the
context of an organisation most people are happy with this one: 'a
team is a group of people working together towards a common and
agreed purpose'. This definition will cover most situations in
schools where team-work is applied to get things done in an effective
and efficient manner.

The next step is to clarify in our minds what are the benefits of
teamwork and to acknowledge that there may be drawbacks too. In
the debate with colleagues who are expressing a distrust of working
in teams it is to the deputy's enormous advantage when she can
demonstrate that the benefits far outway the disadvantages. Try the
following exercise with a colleague or group of staff to confirm this
supposition:

> Divide a sheet of A4 paper down the centre. Label the left-hand
> column *benefits* and the right-hand side *drawbacks*. Brain-storm
> either side in turn. The result should demonstrate to even the
> most cynical that teamwork is an activity worth pursuing.

In carrying out this exercise some of the more common outcomes are
likely to be as shown in Figure 6.1

Benefits	Drawbacks
• shares and spreads expertise	• takes up time
• divides workload	• too many meetings already
• gives ownership	• can create conflict.
• enhances commitment	
• enables personal and professional growth	
• can be fun	
• leads to better informed staff	
• clarifies aims and goals.	

Figure 6.1

Of course, many new deputies will be moving into schools where working in teams is a long-established practice and will not, thankfully, be having to evangelise the joys of teamwork. But even in these enlightened institutions there may well be a team 'resistor' and there will be a need to have a well thought out, persuasive rationale for team work.

Team roles

We have all experienced teamwork in many contexts, both in our professional and private lives and will all have observed the fact that some teams work, in that they achieve their objectives in a way which provides satisfaction for the team and with outcomes that are useful and productive, while other teams fail dismally on both counts. What then are the essential elements of teamwork which have the greatest bearing on the end result?

Certainly the manner in which the team is led and managed will fundamentally effect the effectiveness of the team but there is another aspect which will have equal if not greater importance. This is the composition of the team and the strengths and weaknesses of individuals within the team. It is important to develop some understanding of this chemistry, this dynamic and how members of groups adopt team roles.

In his book *Management Teams: Why they Succeed or Fail* Meredith Belbin (1981) gives a fascinating account of his research into the dynamics and interaction of individuals working together in teams and produces some extremely helpful conclusions for those involved in setting up and managing them. Among the many outcomes of his research at the Henley Management Centre was the work done on team roles. Belbin was able to show that:

- Successful teams contain a balance of team roles.

- Eight distinct team roles can be identified.

- No particular role is more important than another.

- As individuals we have a leaning towards a particular role.

- This leaning may vary according to the work context.

- Certain occupations attract particular role types.

For the purpose of our discussion here the most important of these findings is the fact that within a successful team each individual has equal importance and carries equal weight and that in most situations the most effective teams are composed of a range of role types.

The eight team roles that were identified by Belbin have been widely accepted by others working in the field of management development and training and are worth looking at in detail. Here is a description of the role types with an indication of the strengths and weaknesses of each; they are, of course, in no order of priority.

Team roles and characteristics:

- **The chairperson (CH):**
  - No more than average in terms of intellect and creativity.
  - Pragmatic.
  - Not necessarily the team leader.
  - Displays powers of coordination and control.
  - Operates primarily on a democratic and participatory basis.
  - Ready and able to assume direct control when necessary.
  - Skilled at recognising and using resources in the group; balancing strengths and weaknesses.
  - Focuses on objectives and directs team towards them.
  - Personal style dominant but relaxed, assertive in a non-aggressive way.
  - Displays trust and belief in people; sees individuals' talents as a resource not a threat.
  - Shows enthusiasm outwardly; underneath is reserved detached and objective.
  - Sense of duty, doing things properly; resistant to pressure.
  - Possesses many qualities that underpin other team roles; should adapt these according to team's needs.
  - Strong on ego.

- **Company worker (CW):**
  - Accepts rules, conventions and constraints of the organisation and gets on with the job.
  - Able to translate concepts and ideas into action plans.
  - Conscientious; works with determination and common sense.
  - Dislikes ambiguity and having to be flexible, adaptable or expedient.
  - Self disciplined; high on integrity and sincerity.
  - Distrusts new ideas, experimentation or change.
  - Less effective as team leader; more suited to being solid backbone.

- **Completer-finisher (C-F):**
  - Anxious, compulsive, introverted.
  - Can apply high nervous energy to productive use.
  - Channels worries, fears and compulsion towards com-

pleting tasks to high standards and to deadlines.
- Without a C-F team is liable to: fall behind schedule, make mistakes in details, become complacent, put aside some issues.
- Expresses concern, urgency, by nagging colleagues.
- Dislikes the casual.
- Has strength of character, sense of purpose and self-control.
- Not any easy person to live with; may lower team morale and induce anxiety in others.

- **Team worker (TW):**
  - Sensitive to the needs, feelings and concerns of other team members.
  - Perceives strengths and weaknesses in team and helps promote strengths and underpin weaknesses.
  - High contribution to team morale; facilitates good communication and co-operation.
  - Can minimise friction caused by 'shapers' or 'plants'.
  - Loyal to team; helps defuse conflict and disruption.
  - Often a stable extrovert low on competition.
  - Good at delegating; professional development of others seen as important.
  - Tendency to promote cosiness and harmony when a degree of tension or conflict could be more productive.
  - Sorely missed when absent from team.

- **The shaper (SH):**
  - Leads from the front, guns blazing.
  - Dominant, assertive, extrovert, impulsive and impatient; easily frustrated.
  - Desires to shape team's work personally and directly.
  - Seeks quick results and compliant followers.
  - Shortcuts complex issues with incisive decisions.
  - Pushes self and ideas to get task done and satisfy personal need to be in charge.
  - Dislikes rules and procedures.
  - Quick to criticise while unduly sensitive to criticism; responds emotionally.
  - Tendency to intolerance and highly competitive.
  - As leader will not get the best out of team.
  - When operating well; commands respect, is inspirational and gets things done.
  - Sees team as extension to ego.
  - Works best in an informal setting with equals; less effective within a formal structure.

- **The resource investigator (RI):**
  - Dominant extrovert with restless enquiring approach to life.
  - Able to explore resources and ideas outside team.
  - Has wide range of useful contacts.
  - Characteristics; cheerfulness, enthusiasm, maintains good team relationships.
  - Tends to lack self-discipline and be impulsive.
  - Thrives with variety, challenge and constant stimulation.
  - Low on creativity but able to stimulate ideas in others by introducing possibilities from a broader context than the team.
  - Persuasive and able to motivate others.

- **The monitor-evaluator (ME):**
  - Strong on critical and analytical thinking.
  - Compliment to 'shaper'.
  - Shrewd, perceptive, cautious and objective; has a serious approach.
  - Able to make correct and reliable judgements.
  - Less strong on persuasion and motivation; tends to be over critical and negative.
  - May lower morale and become alienated from team.
  - Keeps team's feet on the ground and pragmatic.
  - Intellectual ability to interpret large amounts of complex data.
  - Competitiveness can lead to group conflict.
  - May over dominate as team leader, stifling process.
  - Tendency to cynicism or overly sceptical.
  - Often seen as having low motivation by team.

- **The plant (PL):**
  - Able to transform team's thinking by presenting innovative ideas and strategies.
  - Usually high intellectual ability coupled with imagination.
  - Self confident, assertive and uninhibited in expressing ideas.
  - Focuses on ideas not people.
  - Radical thinking can ignore practicalities.
  - Ingenuous outlook can lead to unhelpful behaviour in group.
  - Sensitivity to criticism may cause withdrawal from activity.
  - Provides breakthroughs when the process has become stuck.

- Needs careful handling by the chair to fully benefit from undoubted talents.
- Can absorb a good deal of team's energy.
- Becomes bored quickly.

Most people on first coming upon Belbin's work quickly recognise themselves in one of the eight role types. For the reader who is interested Appendix V consists of a 'self perception inventory' which will help identify, or confirm, which role they most closely match. It is as well to remember that the theory indicates that individuals have a leaning towards one type in particular but there will also be strong tendencies shown to one or, sometimes, two others. This self awareness can be useful for the occasions when working in a team there is a need to shift one's role according to the composition of the group or to counter an imbalance of roles.

Armed with this insight into the way that individuals perform within teams what practical benefits may this knowledge bring to the deputy?

At the simplest level it will help explain the behaviour and actions of colleagues when placed within teams and this can also extend to other situations in school where groups of adults meet together, for example governors' meetings, parents' committees, staff meetings and workshops. These are not all teamwork settings but the role types will be operating and the outcomes of these groups will be influenced by the 'role mix'.

As part of the SMT the deputy will be called upon, possibly in collaboration with the head, to create teams or to advise others on their composition. A knowledge of team roles in these circumstances will prove to be a great advantage in determining the success, or lack of success, of the teams. The prime understanding that effective teams contain a cross section of talents and aptitudes will help avoid the common mistake of creating teams from like-minded individuals the end result of which is likely to be a cosy harmony with little creative outcomes. As it is impractical to imagine that each member of staff could be given the test to identify their role type, in fact most would object strongly to any hint of psychometric probing, their strengths and weaknesses as team members will have to be identified by observation and, with some, through discussing their own feelings of their team abilities.

It is evident that the average sized primary school is not going to provide a wide enough range of role types for any kind of perfect team structuring but accepting that each individual will have supplementary, back-up strengths then it is possible to put together teams containing a reasonable mix. Having said this it is worth pointing out that having applied the Belbin questionnaire with a large number of teachers on management training courses there is clearly a predominance of 'team workers' and 'company workers' in the profession!

Team building

Teams will be constructed in schools for a variety of purposes and will have a range of life expectancy. They may be short term, for example to organise a summer fair, medium term perhaps to develop a new policy or long term in the case of a curriculum team. Whatever the purpose or length of time they are in operation they will need to have a method of operating and a system in place to keep them alive; team building and maintenance. Even though teams will fluctuate and change over time in response to the school's developmental needs the personnel within the school will, largely, remain unaltered; in other words the teams will be composed of the same staff in different permutations. It therefore seems logical that a school adopts a common code of practice for teamwork and uses team processes that everyone is familiar with even before new teams are set up. We will now investigate a model process that many schools have adopted and have found highly supportive in teamwork.

A management development and training group which, in recent years, has had considerable influence in the area of teamwork and team development over industrial, commercial as well as educational groups has been the Coverdale Organisation. Its philosophy is based on the premise that teamwork is most effective when the team adopts a *systematic approach* to problem solving and decision making. The essence of the Coverdale training is to bring participants to this conclusion themselves and to practice an established systematic method. What follows is a very much condensed version of this approach which, nevertheless can be successfully applied by deputies in teamwork situations in their school.

The systematic approach is based on a series of logical steps which start with identifying the 'problem' or the 'decision' or the 'outcome' that the team desires and leads through an agreed pathway to achieve the result.

As an aid to remembering the stages in the process the, unmemorable, acronym TOSIPAR is used (see Figure 6.2).

T	–	tuning in
O	–	objective setting
S	–	success criteria
I	–	information & ideas
P	–	planning
A	–	action
R	–	review

Figure 6.2

Taking these step by step:

1. **'Tuning in'**: At the starting point the team needs to very carefully clarify what the task is it is faced with. Complete understanding and agreement of the issues involved are essential at this stage in order to avoid time wasting misunderstandings and hiccups later in the process. If the task has been presented in written form, for example a directive from the DFE or local authority, it is equally important to clarify and agree on the meaning of syntax and key phrases.

2. **'Objective setting'**: 'What are we here for?' and 'What are we setting out to achieve?' Again full agreement and clarity of goals is essential. Unless all members of the team know which direction to go the team is unlikely to reach its destination. It is useful to have agreed objectives recorded. Soundly formed objectives need to be SMART: specific, measurable, achievable, realistic ... and time constrained.

3. **'Success criteria'**: This expression often causes confusion; it simply means agreeing a set of statements which describe what the situation will look like when the objectives have been reached. They should be clear, concise and unambiguous.

Time spent on these three initial steps will save time later on.

4. **'Information and ideas'**: This is where the creative part of the process begins. It will involve discussion, pooling of ideas, uncovering options and alternatives, sharing knowledge and expertise and deciding if outside information and resources are going to be needed.

5. **'Planning'**: Now will be the point at which decisions are taken and an action plan put together to implement these decisions. The 'who does what by when' stage involves

delegation of specific tasks to individual team members with deadlines set for their completion.

6. **'Action'**: This simply means going away and doing it.

7. **'Review'**: The final, and often neglected, stage in the teamwork process which comes when it seems that all objectives have been reached. The aim at this point is to match the agreed success criteria with the attained objectives to see how fully they have been achieved. Also to look back at the whole process and try to identify where it worked well and where mistakes were made.

   This often provides a valuable opportunity for team learning and development. Reflection may lead to interesting questions: 'Why didn't we quite match our success criteria? Was it through poor action planning or poor delegation of tasks? How can we do it better next time?'

This process needs frequent practice until the stages become imbedded in the team's consciousness and are dealt with automatically every time there is a problem to be tackled or a decision to be made.

However, the usefulness of the systematic approach need not be confined to group or team situations. The process can be as helpful for two or three people working together as it is for a larger number; for example the system can be usefully applied by an SMT of head and deputy. It even works with one person alone.

Deputies may wish to try this out for themselves and become familiar with the steps involved before introducing the process into teamwork. A simple starting point is to take an issue, perhaps in their personal life, which is presenting itself as a problem or where decisions have to be taken; this might involve something as non-threatening as where to go on holiday next year. After deciding on a fairly straightforward focus the task is then to take it through each of the stages in the TOSIPAR process to practice the system at first hand. After developing some familiarity with the systematic approach more complex and important issues can be tried, eventually leading to its use with colleagues at school.

Team leadership

From the expertise they will have brought with them to the school, and by the nature of their managerial role the deputy will, inevitably, be regularly drawn into the role of team leader across a range of contexts and involving a variety tasks. Much of what was written about leadership in Chapter 3 will have a direct bearing on how successful is this leadership and how it is best exercised.

Every team leader has a range of responsibilities and tasks and the following agenda can be used by team leaders as an *aide memoire* when reviewing a team's progress and their personal effectiveness in promoting team spirit and leading a successful group.

Questions a team leader needs to ask:

- Is a systematic approach, understood by all, being used?
- Is there mutual respect and tolerance among team members?
- Are individual aptitudes and talents being recognised and used?
- Do individuals feel they have a unique contribution to make?
- Are arrangements made for team meetings always clear to everyone?
- Are team members clear about objectives and action plans?
- Do team members feel free to discuss alternative approaches and solutions?
- Has a climate of trust been established?
- Are there regular review and progress reports?

Positive answers to all, or most, of these questions will indicate that the team is being led effectively and will have developed strong group working practices. Substantial numbers of negative answers will need careful analysis and further questions applied to weak areas that have been identified. Careful consideration will need to be given to whether the concern appears to lie in the area of team process management or people management and appropriate action taken to remedy the difficulties. In this situation enlisting the help of a 'critical friend' to discuss the perceived weaknesses may be a fruitful way forward.

Finally there are some core aspects of leadership that need to be clearly demonstrated to team members. The team leader must be able to show that:

- They know what they are doing.
- They know where they want the team to go.
- They know how they are going to get there.
- They know what each team member is expected to achieve.

Teamwork can be a powerful management tool in the hands of someone who understands the dynamics of the processes that are involved. New deputies will progress rapidly towards their goal of becoming effective school managers when they develop this understanding and are able to operate the processes smoothly and confidently.

7 The management of conflict

A comment often heard being made by senior managers of primary schools when the subject of conflict arises goes something like, 'We all get along together really well and there's never any sign of conflict at all in our school'. This kind of remark either displays a lack of sensitivity to the dynamics of staff relationships or alternatively reveals someone who has a close affinity to the ostrich. Conflict within organisations is inevitable and this fact is our starting point for a chapter whose premise is that conflict can be managed, not just coped with or not just dealt with, and that conflict has positive aspects which may be used to further change and development.

The issues to be spotlighted will be

- Well managed conflict vs poorly managed conflict.
- Conflict and the deputy.
- Approaches to resolving conflict.
- Conflict management strategies.

Well managed conflict vs poorly managed conflict.

As with other sections of this book when opening a window onto fresh management issues we shall begin by clarifying the purposes of managing this area well, as opposed to ignoring its existence or managing it poorly.

Conducting a brainstorming exercise with teacher groups on the positive aspects of conflict against the negative side produces the kind of result shown in Figure 7.1.

Positive aspects: well managed conflict:	Negative aspects: poorly managed conflict:
● Reason and rationality prevail.	● Emotion rules OK!
● Clarifies problems.	● Inhibits change.
● Reveals concerns.	● Encourages factions.
● Enhances professionalism.	● Communication closed.
● Develops problem solving.	● 'Infections' spread.
● Clarifies purpose and aims.	● Outcomes are 'win-lose' or 'lose-lose'.
● Allows challenge.	● Stifles creativity.
● Outcomes are 'win-win'.	● Creates instability.
	● Prevents sharing.

Figure: 7.1

These ideas are mostly self-explanatory and illustrate clearly that a regime which can manage conflict has benefits for everyone in the organisation.

The expression, 'win-lose' simply describes the resolution of conflict where one party, or group, having gained supremacy in the argument or dispute feels it has 'won'. This naturally leaves the opposition feeling it has 'lost' together with all the accompanying negative emotions and destructive 'infections'. The opposite, a well managed resolution leads to 'win-win' outcomes where both sides feel satisfaction and move forward in a degree of harmony. Some of the strategies described later will help deputies towards these benefits and positive outcomes.

Conflict and the deputy

Making the assumption that it takes two to tango, and that at least two parties, or groups, are needed to initiate conflict, it may be generated within schools, from a variety of sources. For example, between children and children, between parents and head, among staff factions, even between deputy and head; the combinations and permutations are seemingly endless. The issues which give rise to conflict will, of course, be quite different depending on the individuals involved but what may help, when reflecting on the multitude of situations that might have to be faced as a deputy, is the fact that the general principles determining conflict management will apply across the board.

From the deputy's perspective experience shows that there are two particular areas of conflict into which they are likely to be drawn and there will be two distinct roles which they will perform; that of *arbitrator* and that of *opponent*.

As *arbitrator* they will be faced with having to manage conflict as a third, neutral, party in disputes arising between individuals or groups within the school. For example, conflict arising from differing perspectives of the school's aims and objectives held by the head and governors set against those of the teaching staff. Of course, in a well managed school where collaborative work and open management is the norm this kind of divergence should be minimal, but, unfortunately, many deputies can find themselves in between two strands of ideas which are pulling in different directions. It may be conflict which has developed between individual colleagues or teacher and primary helper and where the deputy has been approached to help resolve an impasse.This kind of conflict has to be resolved and it is often down to the deputy working with the opposing sides, to tackle the problem and reduce the tensions.

As an *opponent*, the second commonly experienced role, the deputy is in direct conflict with an individual member of staff and this is a problem which may arise at any time during the period of deputy headship. Often the issue at the core of the conflict is quite trivial and it is presented as a challenge to the deputy's authority or position in the management hierarchy; it is in fact essentially a testing out of the deputy. Nevertheless, however trifling the source it will need to be managed effectively to produce a win-win outcome. It may be of small comfort to reflect that it is not uncommon for even the smallest primary staff group to have within its number someone who is universally recognised as being 'a difficult person'. The source of the deputy's conflict will as likely as not come from this individual and they will be one of his/her long line of victims. If and when the deputy is cast in either of these conflict situations they will need some strategies to be able to resolve the problem.

Approaches to resolving conflict

We are all familiar with and have observed the three basic approaches to conflict resolution.

Peaceful co-existence

First, the 'let's not disturb the waters of harmony' philosophy of *peaceful co-existence*, where the chief objective is to find common ground and areas of agreement. Opponents are encouraged to live together and not to rock boats. This tranquil solution to conflict resolution may, on the surface, maintain harmony but can also conceal a mass of frustration and tension over issues which are not given a real airing and discussion which is stifled or constrained. The conflict which has been smothered by this approach is likely to surface at a later date with greater vehemence and create bigger problems than if it had been faced head on at an earlier stage.

Compromise

Second, and equally not to be recommended as a universal approach, is *compromise*. The rationale behind this strategy is the assumption that there is no 'right' answer and that conflict can be resolved through negotiation or bargaining or 'splitting the difference'. The likely outcome through applying compromise is a 'lose-lose' one with neither party feeling much satisfaction. The real issues at the heart of the conflict are again likely to remain unresolved and will fester under the surface of apparent agreement.

Problem solving

The better, and undoubtedly more difficult, approach is through *problem solving* where an attempt is made to face problems head on rather than just taking on board different points of view. In a problem solving approach the core issues of the conflict are analysed through a creative process thus producing the opportunity for positive and lasting change in the situation. The resolution of problems are reached by those directly involved with the issues so generating a commitment to, and an ownership of, the solutions.

A model for the problem solving process has a number of sequences resembling the TOSIPAR method examined earlier:

1. Those involved clarify and agree what is the core problem.

2. Objectives are decided for a solution, i.e. What does each want?

3. Through objective discussion, alternative solutions are listed.

4. Agreement is reached on the preferred solution.

5. An action plan is formulated to implement the solution.

The application of the problem solving approach in dealing with conflict calls upon careful management of the process and needs sensitive chairing or leadership by an impartial third party. This is where the role of deputy as effective arbitrator is often of great influence and importance.

Conflict management strategies

Deputy as an arbitrator

Ideally the involvement of a third party, or arbitrator, should be initiated by the two parties involved in the conflict, in reality, and particularly where the dispute has escalated from a professional disagreement to one which has become personalised, this is unlikely to happen. If a point has been reached where views and attitudes have become set in concrete then it will be necessary for the deputy to take the initiative and set up the arbitration process. Another, not uncommon scenario, is where one party in the dispute approaches the deputy to enlist their support in the conflict. When this happens the deputy must avoid any sign of taking up a side and instead offer to mediate in the hope of resolving the problem. The arbitration process will involve setting up a *conflict solving meeting* which will be chaired by the deputy. If the conflict lies between two individuals then they will obviously need to agree to the meeting and if the dispute involves two opposing factions then for this initial meeting a representative from each group will have to be nominated to attend; it would not be wise to take on the management of whole groups in conflict at this stage.

The conflict solving meeting will need to be led through the following steps:

1. Establishing *ground-rules*; these should include the right to be heard without interruption, sticking to the relevant issues, being honest and objective, acting professionally and compliance to the wishes of the chair.

2. Each party involved is allocated a slot in which to talk openly about the *issues concerning them* during which they are encouraged to state their aims, feelings and views openly and calmly. The chair should attempt to steer this input into a global context, i.e. how the issues relate to the aims and priorities of the whole school not merely those of the individual concerned.

3. The meeting then begins to explore what might be *common goals* for both sides. The focus here is on the future not past

actions and events. The chair's task here is to encourage understanding of opposing views, to discourage defensive or attacking comments and to build on ideas that are generated by the discussion.

4. This discussion will lead to *concrete proposals* agreeable to both parties. These need to be carefully recorded and the action that each of those involved are to take, the 'what, who and when'.

5. A date and time for a *further meeting* to review progress.

The prime purpose of the arbitrator is to keep the conflicting parties strictly to this process and guide-lines and not, themselves, to comment on the issues or offer solutions. In many cases this initial meeting will be enough to break down established barriers and the communication it establishes will lead to a resolution of the conflict. In more complex situations it may constitute only the first of a series of mediation sessions.

Deputy as an opponent

When involved in conflict with another individual, whether it be colleague, parent, schoolkeeper or governor, there are some basic procedures that apply:

- **Deal with the issue as soon as possible:** Quite minor and trivial conflict can develop into worrying and insomnia inducing concerns if they are left to germinate, even overnight. Tackle the problem as soon as it arises.

- **Refrain from talking about the other person:** The discussion of the issue with a third party may feel therapeutic but it has to be done in a professional way which avoids focusing on the other individual concerned.

- **Involve an arbitrator:** If the problem canot be resolved between the two parties at stage one, approach a third 'neutral' person for their help. Someone with whom both sides have confidence.

- **Agree to a conflict solving meeting:** At the meeting stick to the groundrules and carry out the action plan decided.

Another strategy which may be of help, particularly when preparing for a conflict solving meeting, is to go through a role reversal exercise, the purpose of which is to come to a recognition of one's opponent's point of view.

The exercise consists of a series of reflections, which may be recorded or not:

- Why is the other party behaving as they are?
- What pressures are bearing on them?
- What are they trying to achieve?
- What common goals are there?
- What are the possibilities for accord?

The outcomes of this reflection might be taken to a third party to have an objective view given of your reflection. This discussion should, of course, always be conducted at a professional, non-judgemental level and scrupulously avoid personal comments about the opposing individual.

As a consequence of the intense emotional, physical and psychological demands on primary teachers interpersonal conflict within many schools is an unhappy fact of life and the deputy who escapes involvement in it will indeed be fortunate in avoiding what can be quite distressing and energy sapping circumstances. In dealing with this area of management it is supportive to everyone concerned to have procedures established which can be swung into action whenever conflict arises. Some of the ideas presented above could well be used in compiling a set of 'conflict guide-lines' for use with both adults and children.

Part III
The developing role

8 Management tools

Part 3 takes us into the stage where the newly appointed deputy has worked on and grown into a number of areas of school management and wishes to extend their repertoire of strategies, skills and knowledge. This might come about through a widening interest in school management or simply from the increasing demands being brought to bear as a member of the senior management team. Other pressures which might at this stage be influencing changes in their role and responsibilitics could be the appointment of a new head or the loss of senior, experienced colleagues. External demands, from the LEA or The Department for Education could also be impinging on and changing the nature of the job. The increasing complexity and range of management tasks that the deputy will be taking on board will, naturally, call for a corresponding widening of strategies for dealing with the issues that arise. The aim of this chapter is to present a selection of *management tools* that the deputy might take and use in order to manage more effectively.

A management tool is merely a process, procedure or technique which is simple to learn, easy to implement and can be used in dealing with a variety of management issues. We have already looked at one such technique, the TOSIPAR problem solving/decision making procedure and the ideas which follow are mainly concerned with this area but will also include *needs analysis* and *prioritising*.

The tools presented here are to help deputies and teams in their thinking and clarification of problems and change. They will assist the management of the school by:

1. Systematically examining what's going on.

2. Identifying and highlighting 'good' practice.

3. Using this to develop improved practice.

4. Record progress along the path to achieving targets and measurable goals.

They are essentially *thinking tools*.

Many management tools come from the world of industrial and commercial management but nevertheless they are appropriate for our purpose of becoming better school managers. Some procedures, such as brainstorming, are already used extensively within primary schools though sometimes the processes are applied without a very clear understanding of their purpose or the ground-rules that must be applied. These, perhaps familiar techniques, are included here in order to clarify how they are meant to be used. Others may be new to deputies or they might have been involved in their use without fully understanding their application.

Our management tools menu will include:

● Brainstorming.

● The nominal group technique.

● SWOT.

● Matched pairs.

● Force field analysis.

● The five why's.

● The diagnostic window.

Most can be used in large or small groups, with a partner, even individually and within a school or personal context. They all work, given the appropriate context.

Brainstorming

This is likely to be the most familiar technique and one which most of us met first in our Initial Teacher Training and promptly forgot. It is a simple and effective technique, if used properly, and a messy and frustrating one when misapplied.

The purpose of the brainstorm, or, rather inelegantly, the 'brain-dump', is to provide a forum in which ideas can free flow without constraint and where participants are encouraged to be uninhibited in the generation of original ideas. The group can be as small as two or three though a maximum size of a dozen active members is probably the upper limit. The secret of successful brainstorming lies with the leader, or chair establishing a set of ground-rules, clarifying the process and seeing that the group sticks to these.

The ground-rules:

- Everyone has the opportunity, and is actively encouraged, to contribute.

- Contributions may not be discussed, criticised or evaluated during the initial steps.

- Silences are allowable and can produce creative ideas.

- All ideas, however outlandish, will be recorded.

The process:

1. The leader clarifies the issue or problem before the group.

2. The group is reminded of the ground-rules.

3. Ideas, suggestions etc. are invited from individuals each being recorded on a flip-chart without comment from other members.

4. After allowing a reasonable period of time, say 15 minutes, the brainstorm is stopped.

5. The group is allowed to ask for clarification of the contributions where necessary.

6. With the contributors' agreement similar suggestions can be combined.

7. The leader takes the group through a discussion whose purpose is to select the most effective or appropriate ideas.

Brainstorming may be used as a stand-alone procedure, as described above, or it can be used in tandem with another management tool to provide a kick start for prioritising or needs analysis.

Nominal group technique (NGT)

The purpose of this procedure is to enable individuals within a group to put forward ideas, proposals, or suggestions, depending on the nature of the issues that are being faced, and for these contributions to be prioritised in a systematic and equable way.

NGT allows people in quite large groups to feel that they have been able to contribute in the prioritising process and it can be a helpful procedure to use when there is likely to be wide divergence of views. The nature of the technique means that difficult, perhaps contentious, proposals are depersonalised thus enabling less assertive members of the group to put forward their ideas without fear of criticism or attack.

As with brainstorming the group will need to have the steps in the process explained to them, or given a reminder, and made to keep strictly to the process. The times given against each step are merely indicators and can be modified as needs dictate.

The process

The group is faced with an issue and needs to come up with a set of prioritised proposals. This could be posed as a question, maybe something like 'What are our priorities for INSET days over the next 12 months?'

Step 1.   Without conferring each member of the group writes down a list of 3–5 suggestions (7–8 min).

Step 2.   They are then told to prioritise their personal list, giving '1' to the top priority (2 min).

Step 3.   One group member acts as scribe and, using a flip-chart, asks each person in turn to read out their number one priority. These are written for all to see without question or comment. After each has given their first priority the round starts again by asking for second priorities and so on until all the proposals have been exhausted. Inevitably there will be duplicate proposals; these do not have to be written twice (20 min).

Step 4.   The scribe, or chair, checks that each item on the list is understood by all the group. This is purely for clarification, nothing should be removed unless items are duplicated (10 min).

Step 5.   Without conferring each individual votes for the five proposals which they see as top priorities by writing: 1st priority = 5, 2nd priority = 4, etc. (3 min).

Step 6. Each item from the flip-chart list is read out and votes cast by the group members. The scribe then totals the score for each proposal (5 min).

Step 7. Finally the five prioritised proposals are recorded in rank order.

As indicated by the suggested timings for each step in the process the procedure can take up to 40 minutes to complete. This is a considerable chunk of everyone's time so the use of the NGT is usually reserved for important issues and other prioritising techniques may be practised for less weighty questions.

SWOT

This acronym represents *Strengths, Weaknesses, Opportunities* and *Threats*. SWOT is a management tool designed to help identify needs and to indicate areas for possible development. It is a technique that can be used by groups and may also be applied by individuals to issues affecting their personal management responsibilities.

This tool, which comes from the world of marketing, has been found to be an effective starting point for schools setting out to complete a whole school review prior to establishing a new School Development Plan when staff and governors endeavour to identify the school's developmental needs over the coming two or three years. Other staff groups have used it when conducting a curriculum review, the purpose of which is to identify areas of the curriculum that need further development. It may also provide a positive way forward for an individual teacher when analysing an area such as classroom management or their organisation of assessment and recording.

The deputy will find it a useful technique to be able to apply both for their individual needs analysis as well as with groups of colleagues.

The process

1. As with other techniques the starting point must be a clarification of the issues before the group to ensure that a common focus is being held by all involved.

2. For use with a group the framework shown in Figure 8.1 is drawn on a flip-chart or large sheet of paper for everyone to see.

3. Group members are then asked, without discussion to note down what they feel are the strengths, weaknesses,

opportunities and threats inherent in the issue being
focused upon allowing sufficient time for reflection to
enable the responses to be considered and thoughtful.

4. Focusing first on 'strengths', the chair invites contributions
   which are written without comment, under this heading on
   the chart until all suggestions have been exhausted.

5. In the same way responses are recorded next under
   'weaknesses', then 'opportunities' and finally 'threats'.

6. The group will then have before it a composite, and very
   subjective, set of views around the issue. The task of the
   chair is to lead a discussion whose purpose, while
   acknowledging weaknesses and threats, is to guide the
   group towards identifying:
   – **strengths** that can be built upon to compensate for
     weaknesses;
   – **threats** that can be turned into **opportunities**.

7. This discussion, if handled skilfully, will lead to a set of
   suggestions and proposals to be taken forward for
   development. These will need prioritising; one of the
   prioritising tools, 'matched pairs' or the 'Nominal Group
   Technique' could be applied at this point or at a later stage.

Strengths	Weaknesses
Opportunities	Threats

Figure 8.1

Clearly this could be a 'high risk' technique to use in certain circumstances where the discussion of threats and weaknesses may be
explosive, and may produce anxiety and tensions within the group.
It is recommended that until the deputy's confidence in handling

contentious issues is fully established the technique is only applied in areas which feel safe for the deputy and the group.

Matched pairs analysis

This is another technique which enables groups to prioritise sets of proposals in order to move forward in taking action. The tool was first developed in California in the 1970s and has since been adopted by many schools and institutions in the UK, particularly in prioritising issues for Development Planning. It needs a group to make it work and it can be interesting to use it in the classroom with children.

It is essentially a systematic procedure which uses a grid structure and involves making matched comparisons of a number of proposals. In order to clarify and make sense of the technique it will be helpful to take as an example a grid which was completed by a staff group in the process of formulating its School Development Plan (see Figure 8.2). This is followed by a description of the process that led to its completion.

	Home/community links	Review learning resources	School environment	Reading	Staff morale	Communications	Development PE/games	Development creative arts	Team teaching	Cross phase planning	Total score	Rank – order of priority
Home/community links		7	5	2	5	7	6	7	9	6	54	2
Review learning resources	3		2	1	5	5	3	3	4	5	31	9
School environment	5	8		3	6	4	5	6	7	5	49	4
Reading	8	9	7		7	6	7	6	8	6	64	1
Staff morale	5	5	4	3		7	3	3	6	3	39	8
Communications	3	5	6	4	3		5	4	7	3	40	7
Development PE/games	4	7	5	3	7	5		5	7	5	48	5
Development creative arts	3	7	4	4	7	6	5		8	4	48	5
Team teaching	1	6	3	2	4	3	3	2		3	27	10
Cross phase planning	4	5	5	4	7	7	5	6	7		50	3

Figure 8.2

The process

1. The purpose of the task and the technique to be used is clarified by the group leader.

2. A set of proposals or suggestions is generated by the group through brain-storming.

3. Through discussion and by consensus this agenda is reduced to ten items.

4. The ten items are written down the side and across the top of the pre-prepared grid (as illustrated in Figure 8.2).

5. Starting with item one (Home community links) and working across the grid, comparison is made of the first item it meets from the top line (Learning resources). A score is allocated to this pair in terms of their relative importance to the group and on the basis that ten points must be split between the two. This scoring is arrived at through group consensus. In our example it was agreed that 'Home community links' receive seven points and 'Learning resources' three.

6. The group then looks at the next item from the top line (School environment) and matches this with 'Home community links'. In the illustration this has been given a comparative score of '5' against '5'; in other words the two items were seen as equally important.

7. The process continues in this way until the first item 'Home community links' has been matched with all the items from the top line.

8. The next item down, 'Review learning resources' is then dealt with in the same way by comparing its relative importance with each item it meets from the top line.

9. This procedure continues until all the items have been matched.

10. Finally, individual scores across each row are added up and a rank order of priority is achieved.

One of the strengths of this tool is that it enables the group to look at alternatives in a quantitative way in order to reach a decision about priorities. The process, as described above, may appear long-winded but with practice it can be activated quite efficiently and can become a powerful and effective technique. It is advisable to first apply it to a non-contentious area, such as deciding where to go for the staff's end of term celebrations!

Force field analysis

When preparing for a change or when faced with a curriculum area or management process that is going wrong, it can be helpful to look, in a systematic way, at the forces which are *driving* the change or supporting the process against those which are *restraining* the process or opposing the change. A tool for accomplishing this, which was first developed by Kurt Lewin in the 1940s, is called force field analysis.

This technique helps to identify the factors which lie on either side of a state of equilibrium, or status quo, the *drivers* and the *restrainers*, and enable the team to move the situation forward towards a desired change or to a solution to the problem.

The process (times given are merely indicators):

1. Define and clarify the current problem. A useful definition of a problem is the difference between what exists and what is desired (5 min).

2. Clarify and state objectives; what will the desired situation look like and can it be measured? (5 min).

3. Brain-storm the driving forces and opposing restraining forces that are contributing to the problem. These are written directly onto a flip-chart in the form of a balance sheet, i.e. drivers on the left-hand side and restrainers on the right (10 min).

4. The group analyses these forces more fully aiming to identify the most important tensions that are open to development or change (10 min).

5. Action plans or strategies are decided to deal with these tensions (10 min).

The process may sound simple but it can provide a valuable way of solving what appear to be intractable problems and, because it is so visual, can indicate ways of moving forward in a clear and effective manner.

The five why's

The technique is a useful approach to problem solving when the fundamental root causes of the problem are not immediately apparent. The process enables a team to dig below the surface of the problem into a deeper analysis.

The process is simple, as follows:

1. The problem is outlined and clarified.
2. The first why is asked (this is likely to produce the most superficial reason for the problem.
3. Why is asked four more times. This is when a deeper understanding begins and where the fundamental causes of the problem are brought to the surface.

This example, and the comments which follow it, has been taken from *Total Quality Management and the School* (Murgatgroyd and Morgan, 1993) and will serve to illustrate the process in action with an age old issue. A staff team is digging into the causes of this problem: 'A large number, approximately 60 per cent, of parents do not attend parents' meetings'.

1st Why?   They have traditionally not done so.

2nd Why?   They do not see a relationship between their attendance and changes in the performance of their son or daughter.

3rd Why?   Because we use the evening more as a report-on-progress session than as a contracting-for-change session. We do not help them see a connection between their work and the performance of their sons or daughters.

4th Why?   Because we have not trained our staff to develop change and performance contracts with parents and pupils. What is more, staff have not explored the implications of this.

5th Why?   Because systematically improving performance of pupils with the full involvement of parents is not a priority in this school at this time.

'By using the five Why's this team has a better understanding of the problem. It is not simply a technical matter, but a matter of some significant educational importance. Notice that if the team had stopped after the first why (the most typical point for an analysis to stop) it would have been concluded that the problem was to be expected. By going beyond the first why, it now realises that the issue is one which goes to the heart of the performance improvement strategy of the school.'

As a reminder, many management tools can easily be adapted for use in the classroom with groups of children. The five why's technique is particularly suited to this and can be productively applied to problem solving in areas of classroom management where solutions can only be found and acted on with the involvement and co-operation of the children.

The diagnostic window

This is a visual technique which can be used with groups or as a tool for the individual. Its purpose is to identify areas for change or development and it is often applied by senior management teams and governors during the early stages of School Development Planning. The process enables groups to highlight areas in which growth and development is desirable and feasible (do-able) while acknowledging that there may be other needs which at that particular moment in time cannot be tackled. The technique uses a framework which resembles a window with four panes, each rectangle representing, in turn, issues or areas within the school, which are:

1. working well and open to change;

2. not working well and open to change;

3. working well and closed to change;

4. not working well and closed to change.

The illustration which follows will help to make this clear.

The objective of the exercise is, of course, to identify and agree on the items which are 2; not working well and open to change.

The process:

1. The framework is displayed and if necessary its function explained.

2. The team, through brain-storming, or, more effectively by being allowed thinking time to jot down some ideas, offers suggestions for each of the four categories.

3. Through discussion a consensus is reached and a final version of the diagnostic window agreed.

4. The focus moves to the areas which are 'working well and open to change' and if appropriate, these are prioritised in order of importance to the team.

The example, a real one, shown in Figure 8.3 is the outcome reached by an SMT in the early stages of conducting a whole school review and prior to a larger meeting of staff and governors.

Using this tool enabled the SMT to open up a great deal of positive issues and revealed a number of areas which were in need of growth and development. They acknowledged that there were two elements that were not working well, '*playcentre*' and '*difficult member of staff*' and were, for the time being, not open to change. It is important that these kinds of issue are recognised and logged for there will

	Working well	Not working well
Open to change	**A** ● positive attitude of children ● music ● staff/SMT relationships ● internal communication.	**B** ● curriculum development ● parental involvement ● handwriting skills ● Inf/Jun continuity ● resource organisation ● NQT having problems.
Closed to change	**C** ● governor support ● budget management ● premises management.	**D** ● after school playcentre ● 'difficult' member of staff.

Figure 8.3

be a time when it is appropriate to revisit them and seek solutions.

An inherent risk in carrying out this process can be a concentration on the negative aspects of the school and it is a principal function of the group leader to guide the team into self-congratulation and recognition of the positivies as well as into constructive criticism.

Finally, to round up this chapter, the matrix shown in Figure 8.4 will assist the deputy in selecting the right tool for the job in their quest for more effective school management.

Management task		Management tools
Kick-starting and generating ideas	=	Brain-storming
Problem solving/decision making	=	TOSIPAR, the five why's
Prioritising	=	Nominal Group Technique, matched pairs
Needs analysis	=	SWOT, the diagnostic window
Managing change	=	Force field analysis, SWOT, the diagnostic window

Figure 8.4

There will, of course, be management tasks of a complex nature for which it will be useful to apply several of these techniques in an appropriate sequence. For example, School Development Planning might well consist of a number of stages, such as:

1. Needs analysis.

2. Prioritising.

3. Decision making.

4. Managing change.

It is worth reminding the deputy who is interested in trying out these techniques for the first time that a 'softly-softly' approach is recommended.

Experience has shown that by first applying the tool to a fairly lightweight personal issue and starting to internalise the process, then moving onto a 'safe' school situation, perhaps within a small group using a non-contentious issue, provides the confidence developing stages necessary before attempting the technique with a whole staff or dealing with larger or more complex management problems.

9 Mentoring and peer support

A key function of the deputy is that of provider of professional and pastoral support for both teaching and non-teaching colleagues. The deputy's unique position of having one foot in the staffroom while also being part of the senior management team will generate numerous opportunities, and demands, to exercise the skills and techniques of mentoring and peer support.

For the prospective or newly appointed deputy this aspect of the role may at first appear daunting. However, there are two important factors which are worth reflecting on and which may provide reassurance for the anxious post holder.

First, the path which has led to this point of their career will have provided numerous experiences in the area of supporting others and they will personally have been the recipient of all kinds of advice and professional support from day one of their teaching life. In previous posts, in particular as a curriculum leader, they will have had to provide specialist advice and will have been involved in the professional development of others. As an experienced classroom teacher they will have had the responsibility for tutoring students on teaching practice and may even have been given the role of induction tutor for newly qualified colleagues. These experiences, perhaps carrying with them negative as well as positive memories, will provide a valuable background to the new deputy's support role.

The second factor likely to apply in most situations is that new deputies will be allowed a period of settling in to the post before heavy demands are made on them to provide support and advice, a time during which the skills and strategies or mentoring and peer support can be developed.

However, a time will come when the confidence that others will have developed from observing the effective deputy at work and the growth of their self-assurance will naturally lead to increasing requests from colleagues for support and advice.

This will arise through formal arrangements, for example when the deputy is designated by the headteacher as teacher-tutor for a Newly Qualified Teacher or student on teaching practice. Other demands may come from individuals for informal, confidential support, perhaps from a colleague who may be having problems of one kind or another with their class. Outside the immediate, small world of the staffroom deputies are often seen as the first point of call for parents seeking advice and even counselling.

Whatever the context in which the need for support arises the deputy will be helped by having a range of skills and strategies available to apply to differing circumstance. As individual processes these may not provide the complete solution to particular problems but experience will lead the deputy into developing different combinations of strategies to match the demands of the situation.

The aim of this chapter, then, is:

- to find out what mentoring means;

- to explore ways in which the support needs can be identified;

- to examine some practical ideas for mentoring and peer support.

What is mentoring?

At this point it will be useful to clarify what is meant by mentoring in schools as the term is often casually bandied about without too much understanding.

Mentoring is widely used outside education in industry and commerce, the Shell organisation, for example, has a well-established mentoring scheme, which involves the induction and intitiation of newly appointed employees into the procedures and practices of the company. Within education in recent years a centrally funded mentoring scheme has been set up for newly appointed headteachers.

In schools mentoring generally means the positive support that experienced staff (the mentor) offers to colleagues with less experience (the 'protege' or 'mentee'). Mentoring is best seen as a continuous staff development activity which, once the system is in place, happens during everyday school life.

For mentoring relationships to work there are some basic ground-rules that must be established, and these are common in whatever context the mentoring is being applied. They are:

- having a recognised procedure;
- having a clear understanding of the procedure, and each partner's role, by both parties;
- trust and rapport;
- credibility and genuiness of mentor in the eyes of the protege;
- confidentiality;
- the relationship based on the protege's perception of his/her needs, i.e. protege led;
- the mentor possesses a range of inter-personal skills: counselling, questioning, listening, etc;
- positive attitudes towards the procedures from both parties.

Effective mentoring should not involve the mentor in being directive, judgemental, telling and advising or patronising.

The relationship should be free of management hierarchy, and without any aspect of assessment.

Peer support: who needs it?

How are we to identify where the need for support is and how do we decide what the priorities are? As touched upon in the introductory paragraphs some areas of support will have been designated as part of the functions and responsibility of the deputy. Job descriptions will define these and they will commonly include responsibility for the professional development of NQTs and trainee teachers. These can be time consuming and demanding functions and the deputy finding them on their plate is well advised to seek support from agencies outside the school such as the Teacher Centre staff and in the case of students, from the relevant training institution. But aside from these tasks, which are pre-ordained, what indicators will the deputy be looking out for and what situations will bring other needs to the surface?

Here the openness of the 'staff culture', the degree to which people feel comfortable about discussing their difficulties, anxieties and mistakes, will be the determining factor in how visible are the needs. How much of the ice-berg is above the water? In a school culture which inhibits the open expression of individual and group needs the deputy will need to exercise skills of observation and inference during formal and informal discussion and perhaps set up occasions which enable peer support needs to be identified. In addition to routine staff meetings these might include INSET days, after school workshops, curriculum team meetings and conducting a curriculum audit in order to highlight subject-specific problems.

It can be helpful, periodically, and in collaboration with the headteacher and other members of the senior management team, for the deputy to conduct a support needs review. Through a review an agenda of needs can be compiled and prioritised in relation to the developmental needs of the school as a whole, and then by analysing this agenda the kinds of strategies that will be most appropriate to apply can be determined. One way of doing this is to categorise the items by identifying:

- The *who* – who is involved or to whom do the needs relate?
- The *what* – the nature of the perceived need?

The *who* might involve the whole staff, groups or individuals. The *what* will help to identify whether the need falls under skills, knowledge, management or organisation.

Such a review will also ensure that the support needs of the staff are shared between members of the SMT and not left entirely in the hands of the deputy.

Mentoring and peer support procedures

Deputies having these responsibilities will be faced with having to deliver a range of different kinds of support and will need to have a range of approaches to match them. They will include:

- Classroom observation.
- Counselling.
- Coaching.
- Critical friendship.

Classroom observation

We are heading off this section with the potentially difficult and highly sensitive area of classroom observation. This provides a link with the past, when it was likely that, as a curriculum leader, the deputy had some experience of classroom observation, and into their future role as appraiser where classroom observation provides the guts of the appraisal process. It also provides opportunity to combine other aspects of support such as needs identification, targeting a focus, counselling, and action planning for future development. It cannot be emphasised enough what a loaded issue it can be in some schools and the degree to which meticulous preparation and handling is called for.

The procedure is being dealt with here in some detail as it is a key component in the appraisal process which will be addressed in Chapter 11.

To be effective classroom observation needs to be broken down into three activities, each being of equal importance and each being dependent on the others. They are:

1. Preparation.

2. The observation.

3. Feedback.

Preparation

If it has been agreed between the deputy and the colleague concerned that a classroom observation is the way forward, and, of course, without agreement the process is a non-starter, a meeting must be arranged to enable careful preparation.

For time to be saved and the meeting to have clear and decisive outcomes it is recommended that the deputy prepares an agenda of issues to be covered. A typical menu will look like this:

1. To agree the time and place of the observation.

2. To agree on the focus.

3. To agree the method of recording and style of observation.

4. To agree a time and place for feedback.

5. To discuss the lesson's context and any constraints.

Item 1.   This is self explanatory but the other headings need some explanation.
Item 2.   Here the 'focus' refers to the purpose of the observation. Why is the deputy spending this period of time in their colleague's room? One assumes that there has already been some discussion between the two but it is still vital at this point to clarify what is the core purpose. The general objective will be for the observer to wit-

ness something during the observation session which will inform and shed light on the agreed focus and feed into further discussion. The focus will need to be specific and closely defined. Typical examples where classteachers seek support and advice might include: aspects of classroom organisation such as *grouping of children, organisation of resources*, or teaching techniques such as *use of questioning, lesson structure, teacher's use of language, etc.* Other foci could be subject specific and call upon the curriculum knowledge and expertise of the observer.

Item 3.   We will look at methods of recording in detail later in this section. The method that will be chosen will largely depend on the focus; it will be clear that a particular recording technique will be more relevant than others. The 'style' of observation refers to how the observer will act while in the room. This might range from simulating a fly on the wall to being totally integrated within the children's activity. It's very important that this is agreed so that the classteacher will know exactly what to expect during the observation period.

Item 4.   The sooner the feedback meeting can be arranged the better, ideally within 24 hours. The place needs to be somewhere which will ensure a degree of privacy and lack of interruption; difficult to find in most primary schools but the meeting doesn't have to be on the premises.

Item 5.   The classteacher will need to put the activity that is to be observed into some kind of context. For example, why the children are grouped in a particular way, what previous learning or experience they have had of the activity, where this is leading to and what will be the anticipated outcomes of the lesson. Constraints, if any, may include noting limited resources or children with learning or behavioural problems, etc.

By following such an agenda both parties will feel more confident about the forthcoming observation and there should be few unwanted 'surprises'!

The observation

Practical details which will get the observation off to a positive start will, of course, include being in the room at the agreed time and acting, while in the classroom, in the way agreed during the preparatory meeting. The latter can often cause problems, for the children will not have been party to the previous discussions and will consider it bizarre if the deputy, normally a friendly and warm person, seems, while trying to maintain a 'fly on the wall' mode, to be ignoring their existence. This can be overcome by the classteacher giving, prior to the lesson, some explanation of the deputy's visit and this applies equally to any adults, such as the primary helper who may be in the room during the observation.

The core of effective classroom observation is its recording and keeping to the agreed focus. The recording must be appropriate to the situation and the activity being observed or the focus, and the deputy's experience as an observer. It must, at all times, be conducted in an objective and non-judgemental way. There is no 'best' method but the following are commonly used techniques.

Methods of recording

Tally systems. The observer will have to pre-prepare a sheet listing specific events which relate to the focus. For example, if this were to be 'use of questioning' the headings could include: 'Open questioning', Questions to boys', 'Questions to girls', etc. During the observation the observer puts a mark against each of these events each time they happen. This method leads to a factual record but may limit the subsequent discussion.

Open recording. Here the observer uses a blank sheet of paper and either notes down key points, or, using a form of shorthand, writes quickly recording what is happening. This is sometimes referred to as *verbatim recording* or *script taping*. This method will help in analysing the lesson's structure in later discussion. An alternative way to conduct this is to have made a prior agreement for note taking under relevant headings. Open recording must be factual with interpretation being left for the feedback session.

Timed systems. A sheet is prepared with predetermined timed intervals written down the left-hand margin; these could, for example, be in two- or three-minute intervals. During the observation the observer notes down what is happening at each time point. This may be refined by deciding, in advance, specific categories of events to be noted. This method supports factual recording and can provide useful information for a discussion about lesson dynamics and structure.

Prompting questions. During the preparatory meeting questions are formulated relating to the focus as an *aide-mémoire* for the observer. For example, if the agreed focus were to be 'classroom talk', prompting questions could include: 'Who initiates talk?' 'Which groups of children are contributing most?' 'What is teacher doing to help enrich and extend the talk?' etc. Observer responses in this method are clearly going to be more subjective but careful framing of the questions can help overcome this tendency. There must be a clear, shared, unambiguous understanding beforehand of the purpose of the prompting questions by the two people involved.

Drawing a diagram. The observer, in collaboration with the classteacher, draws a plan view of the classroom indicating where individual children are situated and resources are positioned. The observation can be carried out in a number of ways dependent on the focus. A straightforward example would be to use this method to analyse the way in which children access materials and resources by tracing the routes children take around the room, perhaps highlighting possible rearrangements the teacher may want to consider. A second use for this approach would be in creating a picture of pupil involvement during an activity. To do this the observer writes a code number against each pupil each time he or she interacts with the teacher. The responses, with their code, could look something like this:

1. Answers a question voluntarily (v).

2. Answers a question when asked (a).

3. Asks a question (q).

4. Makes a comment or gives a view (c).

5. Is disruptive (d).

This list of techniques is not, of course, prescriptive and each is open to modification to suit particular situations. Elements of each may also be combined to produce hybrid methods such as the example shown in Figure 9.1, which combines *verbatim recording* and timing and enables the observer to raise queries during the feedback session. The observer simply prepares a sheet of A4 paper in the three columns.

| **Focus of observation:** 'Class management at start of day' | | |
Time	Activity notes	Query
9.05 am	Children begin entering room	
9.07 am	Teacher talking to two parents	Is this fairly usual?
9.09 am	Most children on mat	
9.11 am	Registration starts	Why is JB at this desk?
etc.		

Figure 9.1

A factual account of the activities conducted during the session will provide the observer and the classteacher with useful material and lead the classteacher to reflect on their practice and its effectiveness.

At the end of any classroom observation it is most important that the observer makes a positive comment to the classteacher before leaving the room; we have all experienced that limbo of uncertainty when a visitor to our room has left without a word!

Feedback

Feedback will have it greatest benefits if it is conducted within the following guide-lines:

- it is given within 48 hours;
- it is based on careful and systematic recording;
- it is based on factual data;
- this factual data is interpreted in relation to known and agreed criteria (the focus);
- the interpretation comes initially from the person 'observed';
- it is given as part of a two-way discussion;
- it leads to the development of strategies for building on what has been learned.

Poor feedback is rushed, judgemental, impressionistic and one-way.

These guide-lines apply equally well to situations other than classroom observation and provide a framework for managing what, for both parties, may be a difficult and sensitive situation.

The skills that the deputy will need to exercise are akin to those of counselling and the following, more detailed, description of giving feedback can well be applied to other counselling or supportive one-to-one interactions.

The phrase that is commonly used to describe feedback which will lead to the recipient moving forward and being able to build on the experience is 'constructive feedback'. This, of course, implies that there is another kind of feedback: 'destructive', which, in the hands of an unskilled or insensitive observer, leads to feelings of frustration and hopelessness. Effective, constructive feedback will need to take on board these strategies:

Begin on a positive note.   Start by telling the classteacher what you liked and what went well during the observation. It is a widely held, and largely justified, feeling among teachers that praise from colleagues or senior management is a rare commodity. We all have a tendency to emphasise negative aspects of our work; to focus on weaknesses rather than strengths. Starting with positive remarks will help the classteacher to take on board, and act on, less positive points that may be coming later.

Own the feedback.   Throughout the feedback it should be emphasised that the comments being made and the views being expressed are solely based on the experience of the observation. It should be made clear to the receiver of feedback that what is being said does not represent some universal truth. To avoid the impression that judgements are being made it is helpful for the observer to preface statements with 'In my view'.

Maintain objectivity.   The whole purpose of the recording during classroom observation was to facilitate the collection of factual data and this approach must be carried forward into feedback. Subjective statements such as 'The lesson was excellent', or conversely, 'The activity was dreadful', will produce the corresponding good and bad feelings but they will not enable any learning to begin or encourage any reflection. What the recipient wants to know is what was observed which led the observer to think 'excellent' or 'dreadful'. General comments must be avoided, constructive feedback focuses on the specific. Describing what was observed and saying what effect this had on the observer is a better way of illustrating incidents rather than just stating 'that was good' or 'that was poor'.

For example, 'The way you described the magnetic field to the third group really moved them forward in their understanding'.

Offering negative feedback.   This does not mean simply criticising. The statements that are made, always based on factual evidence, should aim to steer the discussion towards the exploration of alternative ideas or solutions. For example, 'After you had finished your introduction to the activity I counted twelve children who clearly hadn't understood your instructions. How might you change your introduction next time?'

Negative feedback should focus on things which are open to change and that are within the power of the recipient to make that change. There is no mileage at all, for example, in commenting on poor materials or resources when their provision is not within the power of the classteacher.

Winding it up.   The end of a feedback session needs to be carefully handled. If negative issues have been dealt with then it is important to finish with a review of the positive aspects of the observation. However, the observer needs to avoid the classteacher feeling that they have been offered the traditional 'feedback sandwich', i.e. *positive: negative: positive*!

Points which have arisen during the discussion which may lead to growth or change will need to be summarised with perhaps a brief agreement on an action plan for the classteacher to take forward.

This then concludes the description of classroom observation procedures. We have been through the process in some detail for, as stated earlier, when carried through carefully it can become a powerful instrument for support and professional development.

Further strategies for peer support

Counselling. It must be emphasised here that the counselling that
the deputy could become involved with is clearly not that of the psy-
chotherapist and unless they have received the appropriate training
they should keep well clear of such approaches. Perhaps a better
word to describe this kind of support would be 'consulting'.

Counselling can be effective when the deputy is approached by a
colleague with a specific problem. These are often found to be
related to inter-personal problems within the staff group and have to
be handled with the utmost care and discretion. The prime aim of
counselling is to enable the person receiving the counselling to find
their own solution to their problem.

What should be happening during counselling? The deputy who
counsels does not take over the problem from their colleague, in fact
they help him/her to take full responsibility for it and are happy to
withdraw as soon as this is possible. The counsellor never offers
advice and never criticises. They believe that the receiver knows
what is best for him/herself and helps them to discover what this is.
The counsellor spends more time listening than talking and uses
skilful questioning to help explore and analyse the issue in all its
aspects.

A counselling style of support focuses more on the person seeking help than on the problem itself, which means that the counsellor need not have detailed or specialist knowledge about the problem
or issue. The knowledge that is important during the process is the
understanding of human behaviour and the possession of sensitivity
for and empathy towards others.

Counselling skills

1. **The use of language:** The effective counsellor will use
   phrases such as: 'What seems to be the problem?', 'Why do
   you find that worrying?', 'What do you think?', 'How did
   that make you feel?', 'Would you like to tell me more about
   that?' etc.

2. **Communicating:**
   - Body posture: sitting with an open posture facing the
     receiver rather than side by side, legs and arms
     uncrossed, leaning forward slightly.
   - Non-verbal: keep eye contact while avoiding a
     continuous stare, use head nodding to affirm what is
     being said, use facial expression to register interest,
     understanding or puzzlement.

- Verbal: help the speaker to focus by drawing them back to what seems to be the core issue, encourage 'opening up' by using short expressions like, 'Yes, go on', 'And?' etc., use clarifying questions, as above (1).

Above all else the key to successful counselling lies in developing listening and questioning skills which can only be done by 'doing'. For those deputies who may feel that what has been outlined above is foreign to them or lies beyond their present level of skills or confidence then a specialist course of training is recommended. Most institutes of higher education will have on offer courses aimed at teachers who wish to develop this area of their professional life.

Coaching.   This is simply one person giving guidance to another; for obvious reasons the donor of the guidance will be someone having the greater level of experience or skills. It is a core aspect of the whole mentoring process and begins through a demonstration of a particular skill, technique or procedure by the coach in order to demonstrate good practice. The 'protege' then replicates the skill or technique while being observed by the coach; this might well be through classroom observation. The third stage involves the coach giving constructive feedback which will lead either to a further demonstration by the coach or a repetition of the activity by the protege who will aim to introduce modifications resulting from the feedback discussion.

Critical friendship.   This expression has been used on several occasions throughout the book and some explanation will be helpful. Critical friendship describes a professional relationship between two peers where the key features are honesty, trust, confidentiality and mutual respect. It is a two-way arrangement which depends on mutual support. It is not an easy relationship for deputies to establish, for in the truest meaning of the word they will not have a peer within the staff group, and their senior management role could inhibit a completely open exchange of views. Having a critical friend enables each member of the pair to open up difficult or sensitive issues and expect to receive straightforward and honest responses from the other. A practical example might be the disclosure to a critical friend of a proposed action plan. The critical friend would be free to express their opinion of the feasibility of the plan without inhibition and might be asked to help monitor and evaluate its future progress and outcomes.

   This chapter has looked at the deputy's role in providing support on a one-to-one basis. This will not be the only way in which they will be called upon to provide opportunities for staff development and the next chapter will deal with the deputy's role as provider of training and INSET for the whole staff.

10 INSET and staff development

Over the past decade primary schools have made huge shifts in the way in which they deal with staff development and INSET (in-service education and training). The forces and influences which have wrought these changes are too numerous to list here but the overall result has been that schools now have to consider the provision of INSET with greater seriousness. For example, the funding, monitoring and evaluation of training under Local Management has introduced a level of accountabilty that did not exist ten years ago. One consequence of these changes has been the need, even in small primary schools, to have someone co-ordinating the whole area of INSET. Who else, naturally, does the responsibility fall to but the deputy head.

Before moving into the management and organisational aspects of the subject a useful starting point is to clarify the purposes, aims and goals of practicing INSET and staff development.

In 1987 the Advisory Committee on the Supply and Education of Teachers wrote:

'**The case for INSET...**
The case for INSET rests on the needs of the education service, of individual schools and of teachers themselves. First, it is, we hope, common ground that the education service needs an up-

to-date, well trained teacher force contributing to effective curricula change. Second, individual schools need a vital and committed staff, working to agreed goals in a climate which encourages effective developments in curricula change and teaching quality. Third, teachers themselves need opportunities for INSET as part of their personal and professional development. The needs of the education service, of individual schools, and of individual teachers are, of course, closely interrelated. They call for a wide range of INSET activities and flexibility of response.'

The committee's report then went on to identify the prime purposes of INSET which, summarised, are:

- to provide for and invigorate the personal and professional development of teachers;

- to enable teachers to change or expand their range of teaching skills;

- to help teachers in the assimilation of organisational and structural change;

- to put curriculum change and development into the hands of teachers;

- to develop a greater understanding of the needs of the wider community;

- to enhance the knowledge and understanding of school management.

These include some weighty and indeed lofty ideals which perhaps on an initial look feel somewhat distanced from the day-to-day experience of the primary deputy. However, by taking a closer look at the INSET and staff development activities that schools routinely deal with throughout an academic year, this list of purposes will come alive and we can see that each INSET day or workshop or out of school training session will fall under one or other of the purposes.

So much then for the views of those outside the immediate school situation. What will concern us now is how the deputy acting in the role of co-ordinator or leader is going to organise and implement INSET and how within the large agenda of other responsibilities it is going to be managed.

The remainder of this chapter will address the following INSET issues:

- Approaches to INSET: a range of options.

- Building a school INSET policy and a model policy.
- INSET funding.
- Needs identification.
- Organising an INSET day.

Approaches to INSET: a range of options

For some teachers experience has led to a belief that there are two kinds of INSET; one resembles an extended staff meeting with a few sandwiches thrown in at lunchtime and the other is where the head-teacher has been persuaded that it is a good idea that they go off to a grim old school building, euphemistically called the Professional Development Centre where they are talked at for an hour and a half by someone who knows less about assessing Technology at Key Stage 2 than they do themselves.

This, of course, is a caricature of approaches long abandoned but it is true to say that there is still a widely held belief that training or staff development can only happen on courses organised away from the workplace. It is this mind-set that needs to be replaced by an understanding that professional and personal growth can happen under a wide range of circumstances and situations.

An awareness of the diversity of provision of INSET that is available is important in order that the deputy will have a range of options to suggest to colleagues.

The options available are usually gathered into three groups under the, not very elegant, headings of: 'On-the-job', 'Close-to-the-job', 'and Away-from-the-job'.

On- the-job   These are, of course, experiences received while actually undertaking the task of teaching .They would include, the learning and development that occurs in team-teaching and the organisational skills that are developed through working in curriculum teams, self-appraisal involved with the appraisal process, and the growth that can come through classroom observation. A review and reorganisation of individual job descriptions may also lead to increasing self-awareness and the need to manage change. Another activity which can be placed under this heading is the involvement of an advisory teacher working alongside the classteacher, helping them to develop and apply the use of new resources or alternative teaching methods. As INSET co-ordinator the deputy will need to have a knowledge of who the local advisory teachers are, where they can be contacted and what the procedure is for bringing them into the school. Of course, it is a sad fact that, currently, in many LEAs the advisory team is virtually non-existent.

The deputy's role in on-the-job staff development is first to act as a catalyst for the activity, second to give encouragement and to show interest and third to perform the function of reflector and counsellor for the teacher's own review and evaluation of the experience.

One of the chief advantages of this approach is that it involves few resources other than the additional time allocated to review and discussion. A second benefit is that it is tailored exactly to the needs of the individual teacher. On the deficit side there is limited opportunity, aside from the interaction with advisory staff, for the injection of new ideas or the introduction of new strategies and skills.

On-the-job training can be usefully combined with away-from-the-job training, for example on management training courses, where new knowledge and concepts received from trainers can be tried out in the form of school-based assignments back at the chalk-face.

Close-to-the-job   Staff development activities under this heading will usually take place on the school site though not during teaching contact time. They will take the form of:

- working with colleagues in preparing a workshop or demonstration, perhaps as a follow up to an external course;

- paired reading of new publications with a colleague in preparation for a curriculum development or policy change;

- being one of a critical friendship pair;

- role swapping, class swapping;

- being actively involved in whole-school INSET days and training sessions run by colleagues;

- being pro-active in team-work;

- work shadowing, or working alongside, a peer or senior colleague;

- acting as an observer in another's classroom;

- accepting a lead role in whole-school activities, i.e. taking assembly or singing practice

- acting as a specialist consultant for a curriculum area.

Many of these activities will be seen by teachers as something they do routinely as part of their job in which case the deputy's role will be to give feedback and help them evaluate how effective they are in their implementation. The deputy might suggest different approaches and even coach their colleagues in new techniques and strategies. For example, the deputy may need to demonstrate their own skills as a team leader to teachers having difficulties in running their curriculum team, or they may be asked to provide some techniques for recording a classroom observation for someone acting as an appraiser for the first time. Others who need to be moving outside the confines of the classroom will need encouragement and tutoring before they feel confident enough to tackle some of these encounters. For instance, running a workshop or staff meeting for the first time can prove to be an extremely worrying prospect for many teachers and the deputy will perhaps need to provide the novice with an outline of the strategies and structures which can lead to effective meetings management.

As the lead person for staff development the deputy needs to establish a system for monitoring what close-to-the-job opportunities are available within the school and periodically to identify and record who is doing what. This will enable them to gently guide the more reticent members of staff into a wider range of enriching and self-developing activities.

As with all the deputy's actions as INSET co-ordinator there must be close and regular consultation with the headteacher and other members of the SMT within whose province many of the opportunities will lie.

Away-from-the-job   By definition this INSET will take place away from the school and increasingly, outside school hours. The range of opportunities under this heading is considerably wider and more varied than those of the two just discussed. They will include:

- long and short courses;

- award-bearing courses;

- secondments;

- school and specialist centre visits;

- private study;

- specialist support groups.

It follows that with a greater diversity of options the deputy will have to develop a wide knowledge base of these opportunities .

Two important people they will need to get to know are the local inspector within the LEA with responsibility for staff development and the key person at their local Professional Development Centre (PDC). The first task will be to make them aware of the deputy's role as co-ordinator within the school and to ensure that they become the recipient of the programme of INSET events that is being offered. Secondly to lock into any INSET co-ordinators network that may be available locally.

Deputies will need to set up a system to monitor course publicity coming into the school from other sources, such as HE institutions, and ensure that these opportunities are well displayed within the staff room.

The local authority may have set procedures for administering grants to teachers wishing to take up further full-time study. Although it will not be in the power of the deputy to sanction these they will need to be aware of their availability and the procedure for making an application. This also applies to any systems established for seconding teachers out of the school.

In order to be able to advise colleagues wishing to make visits to other schools, perhaps to see a parallel class in action, or teachers wanting to look at resources and materials at a specialist centre it is important that the INSET co-ordinator keeps a record of where these classes might be and who will be the most appropriate contact at a particular centre. This is not a simple task and is best done through the INSET Inspector, the head of the local PDC or during informal discussion with other deputies or INSET co-ordinators at network meetings.

With all off-site activities it is important that someone within the school is logging who is involved in them and what they are doing; clearly the person best placed to do this in this case is the deputy.

Taking our three headings together it can be seen that there is a vast range of INSET activities that the deputy can suggest colleagues might pursue. We will next look at systems for managing them.

A school policy for INSET

As in many other areas of school management the establishing of an agreed policy can be of inestimable help for the co-ordinator or leader who has the responsibility for that particular aspect of school life. There is a paradox associated with INSET and staff development in that while the need for more teachers to receive more INSET is growing the resources, time, money and external support are, in most cases shrinking. The tension which this creates within the school may be awkward for the SMT and in particular the INSET co-ordinator to handle. This may be manifested in the competing demands made by individual teachers for personal and professional development opportunities which will often not match the development needs of the school as a whole, and even further by the external demands for change being made by the LEA or the DFE.

The raft that the deputy will find useful to cling to here will be that of the INSET policy! The inherent value of having a policy statement is that it can be given to all staff and governors so that everyone has a clear and unambiguous picture of the purpose of staff development, the opportunities that are available and, most importantly, the priorities and procedures to be followed.

The formulation and writing of policies was dealt with in Chapter 3 and the procedures outlined there will apply to the setting up of an INSET policy. What will be of help here is to identify the core elements of such a policy and then see an example of an established policy.

A simple structure for the policy could be:

1. Rationale.

2. Purposes.

3. Guide-lines.

The *rationale* and *purposes* might have a good deal in common with other primary school policies while at the same time reflecting the particular needs of that school. Discussion among groups of teachers produces the following kinds of conclusion.

A school policy for staff development should help to improve the effectiveness of the whole school as well as developing the professional skills of individuals. It should therefore set out agreed procedures for meeting and balancing:

- the needs of individual teachers for professional training at different stages of their careers;
- the needs of the school and the related training and support required by staff.

The *guide-lines* might be sub-headed thus:

- Who for?
- Needs analysis.
- Entitlement/access.
- Responsibilities.
- Procedures.
- Feedback/evaluation.

The example shown in Figure 10.1 is of an established, working, staff development policy.

Policy Statement: staff development

Rationale

Staff development and training is a key area of school development. Effective staff development increases motivation and job satisfaction for all staff. It enhances good learning and teaching and the personal development of both teaching and non-teaching individuals. All staff have the right to participate in a clearly defined and agreed development and training programme.

Purposes

1. To support the agreed School Development Plan by extending understanding of and commitment to whole-school policies.
2. To ensure the continuing development of professional knowledge and skills of all members of staff.
3. To anticipate and prepare for educational change.
4. To encourage individual staff to plan their career development and to identify and exploit career opportunities.
5. To share good practice within the school.
6. To ensure entitlement to training for all staff.
7. Through the above, to improve school effectiveness by enhancing the overall quality of teaching and learning in the school.

Guide-lines

1. The responsibility for staff development and training rests with the INSET co-ordinator.
2. The annual INSET consultation will form the basis for implementing the policy.
3. The policy will reflect the school and individual aspects of training.
4. An annual INSET budget will be set. Allocation of this funding will be based on priorities detailed in the SDP.
5. All INSET allocations and expenditure information will be made freely available.
6. Individuals benefiting from training will be responsible for feeding back to colleagues and evaluating their experiences.

Figure 10.1

There are one or two interesting points to note in this example. First responsibility for INSET is clearly in the hands of the co-ordinator at this school. However, other schools may want to spread the load and appoint an INSET committee or even have the responsibilities handled by the senior management team. Secondly it states that an annual INSET budget will be set. This is an essential element to include and implement in the management of INSET.

The structure of the policy doesn't correspond exactly to the 'policy for policies' exemplar discussed in Chapter 3 and illustrated in Appendix II, and the reader might try comparing the two; could this INSET policy benefit from a reshaping and, perhaps, include some additional aspects not included in our model?

INSET funding

Before the widespread introduction of a lead person for INSET into primary schools staff, this area was usually a responsibility taken on by headteachers and due to their heavy workload was often given a low priority in the list of tasks that needed to be done. As a consequence INSET, particularly in the area of funding, was often characterised by being unplanned and *ad hoc*, unrelated to the wider needs of the school, unmonitored and cost ineffective, unfair in that he or she who shouted loudest reaped the benefits, and wasteful of time and money.

A more rational approach to funding, being promoted here, will aim to reflect:

- forward planning and thinking;
- equal opportunities and fairness;
- the school's vision and Development Plan;
- value for money;
- individual teachers' needs;
- creative approaches to providing additional funding/resources.

The deputy tackling the management of funds for INSET will find that there are three fundamental issues that have to be understood and organised, they are:

1. Where's it coming from?
2. Where's it going to?
3. Are we getting value for money?

Sources of INSET funding

Some of what follows will not apply to all schools owing to local differences in practice and interpretation by LEAs and governing bodies on the allocation of central funding, but Deputies will find there will be some commonality between individual institutions.

GEST (Grants for Educational Support and Training)

A substantial proportion of funding will come into schools through GEST (Grants for Educational Support and Training). This is a mechanism that the Government, through the DE, has established to distribute centrally-held funds for the training and development of serving teachers, via local education authorities, to the end user, the individual school. A word of caution here, for over the past three or four years GEST has been radically modified and considerable doubt now hangs over its future. No doubt, however, while central Government still espouses a belief in the need for the professional development of the teaching force, and the flow of new educational initiatives continues, there will still have to be some way of organising the distribution and monitoring of funds. Put simply, GEST consists of a number of categories or areas in which the DE perceives a need for development or training; these have included, senior management training, training for governors, the development of specific curriculum areas, 'end of Key Stage' assessment training, the introduction of teacher appraisal, etc. Individual LEAs have to bid for funds under each of these headings and after a lengthy process are informed by the DE of their allocation. The bids submitted by the LEA will have defined how the funds will be distributed and how their spending will be monitored.

In the past some of the allocation was used to provide a support service, specialist inspectors, advisory teachers, a Teachers Centre, and the remainder distributed to individual schools on a pro rata basis. This is changing, however, for it is the will of the DE that a greater part of GEST funds go directly into schools' budgets where decisions for spending can be made to greater effect and meet individual needs at a local level.

Whatever system replaces GEST in the future it will be important that INSET co-ordinators have a thorough understanding of its working, be clear about the entitlement of their organisation and the procedures required to access the funding.

School budget

As a member of the SMT, the deputy should have close involvement in the setting of the annual budget and, in many cases, will be a member of the governing body's finance committee. Wearing their INSET hat at the same time will enable them to ensure that a portion of the budget is ear-marked for spending on staff development. The purpose of this spending will largely be determined by the needs defined in the SDP but there will be a role for the deputy to play in ensuring that the allocation for INSET is adequate to match predicted needs.

A creative strategy to apply in the case of underspend, on either the school's global budget or the more specific INSET budget at the end of a financial year, is to 'forward fund' the surplus. This means paying in advance for training or support services for the following financial year. Most HE institutions and other providers are more than happy to do this and are willing to leave the focus of the training to be decided at a future date as the needs emerge. Needless to say forward funding has to be carefully recorded for future auditing.

LEA funded

To repeat yet again that the world of LEAs, their roles and functions, is in a constant flux and in the hands of future political changes, is tedious but necessary. Currently there are still some authorities which are providing support services as they have done in the past, and for those deputies working within them it is important to lock into the relevant personnel and communication systems in order to be aware of specific funding that will periodically surface in support of staff development. Very often this kind of funding is allocated by schools through applications or bids and there needs to be close collaboration between the head and INSET co-ordinaor to ensure that these opportunities are not missed.

As previously described LEAs have traditionally held funds for the support of teachers wishing to take courses aimed at advancing their professional qualifications. These take the form of grants and awards, and authorities offering this funding will have a set procedure for teachers to make applications together with a number of criteria that have to be satisfied. The deputy/INSET leader will need to know if this kind of funding is in place locally and if so how their colleagues may access it. The local Professional Development or Teachers' Centre staff should hold this information.

Business/industry

There are a number of schemes run in collaboration with business and commercial organisations which schools can access. They are generally speaking not well publicised and the opportunities on offer are not too numerous. They are of a work experience or work shadowing nature, where the teacher involved leaves their class for a week and joins the organisation either in an active or observational role. Businesses and organisations which have supported this initiative in the past have been Marks and Spencers and branches of the major banks. Teachers, including heads and deputies, who have been involved in these arrangements, which generally focus on management roles, have found them extremely valuable experiences. The most widely known of these schemes is run by the Teacher Placement Service, and many LEAs will have someone attached to them who will co-ordinate and organise the placements.

Local TECs (Training and Enterprise Councils) are government-funded organisations which a few schools have found to be useful sources of training. This seems to be unexplored territory which might be worth investigating.

Self funding

An increasing and unfortunate trend in the area of INSET funding over the past two years has been the number of teachers who, mainly due to shrinking school budgets and the shift of focus to whole school needs rather than the needs of individuals, are funding their own professional development. If individuals are put into this corner by lack of training monies there must be some form of support offered by the school. A common arrangement is for the school to pay for supply cover while the class teacher is away at the course which they have personally funded

HE institutions and other training establishments have become aware of this problem and, particularly in the field of management training, are offering courses which take in weekends and school holiday periods; the 'cost' here being, perhaps, the peace of mind of the teachers involved!

Needs identification

Much of what was written in Chapter 9 on the identification of individual needs for mentoring and peer support will apply equally well here.

Two additional and extremely influential factors will be:

- short- and long-term needs resulting from teacher appraisal;
- needs arising from the School Development Plan.

These, of course, should not be in conflict for there should be a strong link between the two demands in a well managed appraisal scheme.

The final prioritising of needs should not be left up to the INSET co-ordinator but must involve the head and other members of the SMT. However, what the co-ordinator can establish, on an annual basis, is a systematic review of training needs.

Reviewing INSET needs: a procedure

1. Consult individual teachers on their perceived needs, putting it within the framework of the SDP and opportunities available. This can usefully be done through the use of a questionnaire.

2. Invite groups of staff to consider their particular needs, i.e. the nursery team, primary helpers etc.

3. Ask senior staff to review their needs, including whole-school needs raised by an inspection or curriculum audit.

4. Consult governors on their views of the organisation training needs.

This exercise will provide a considerable amount of material which the co-ordinator will need to organise, analyse and present to the SMT for discussion and final decision making and prioritising.

Organising an INSET day

Out of the five statutory INSET days that schools are required to implement, one or more will inevitably fall onto the INSET co-ordinator's shoulders; if all five have to be taken on board then there is something seriously wrong with the school's management structure or, alternatively the person concerned needs intensive training in the skills of delegation. The deputy having this role will first need to demonstrate that they are able to plan and implement an effective training day and second be in a position to advise and support others when it becomes their responsibility.

As in many other management activities we have looked at previously there are a number of stages in the organisation of an INSET session, be it an after school workshop or a whole day's training. These are:

1. Planning.

2. Preparation.

3. Implementation.

4. Evaluation.

To bring this exercise to life we will use a real-life case study to illustrate the progress of the operation and will take the not uncommon theme, a review of the school's Record Keeping and Assessment Policy following a whole-school inspection.

Planning

Planning will be more fun and the outcome will be more stimulating if it is carried out in a small team. In our case study this is likely to be the curriculum co-ordinator for assessment and record keeping and the INSET co-ordinator.

The purpose of the planning, done over a series of meetings will be to:

- Establish the aims and outcomes of the day: what skills, knowledge and understanding will people have at the end of the day?

- Clarify the audience: who are we targeting during the INSET? Will it be appropriate to include non-teaching staff, admin, governors?

- Levels: what is the experience/knowledge base-line that we will be starting at?

- Content: what will be appropriate and feasible to offer during the time available?

- Draft pragramme: what are established training practices? What will people feel comfortable with ? To what degree can new ways of working be introduced to provide interest and stimulation?

- Venue, date times: is the staffroom always the most suitable location?

- Creature comforts: refreshments and lunch; who will provide them? Go out or stay in?

- Human resources: what internal expertise is available? Will external input be necessary?

- Cost: how much is going to be needed from the INSET budget to fund the day?

- Action plan: who has to do what and by when?

Many of these items will be dealt with fairly speedily and won't raise the need for much discussion. Perhaps what would be useful here is to take a closer look at programming the day, for much of the success of the event will hinge on this.

If the aims and expected outcomes have been thought through carefully then the programme will need to be designed to match and provide for them and some understanding of aspects of adults as learners will help in the building of an effective programme.

The prime awareness that needs to be kept at the forefront of the planner's mind is that adults learn best when there is an element of concrete experience in the session and that this can provide a good launching point. Second, many of us have fairly short-term spans of concentration and may become bored with long periods spent in one activity. Third, teachers in particular do not appreciate training that is based entirely on 'learning through discovery' or reinventing a well-worn wheel; they will appreciate the voice of an expert or skilled practitioner somewhere along the line. The approach to training that is widely regarded as the most effective is that of experiential, reflective learning and a theoretical model of this can be seen in Appendix VI, Kolb's experiential learning cycle.

Bearing these thoughts in mind let us return to the Record Keeping day that we started with and see how a programme might shape up:

Draft programme for INSET day

9.00 am	Coffee
9.15 am	Introduction to the day; aims, purpose and hoped for outcomes {deputy}.
9.25 am	Review of the present policy/procedures {assessment co-ordinator}.
9.40 am	Form into groups of three with own record keeping samples, to examine 'what works well, what doesn't work in practice?'
10.00 am	Whole group discussion and recording of findings.
10.30 am	Coffee.
10. 45 am	Input from external specialist in record keeping and assessment: 'Current developments'.
11.30 am	Questions and discussion.
12.00 noon	Lunch.
1.00 pm	Reflection on the morning and briefing for the afternoon (deputy).
1.15 pm	Workshop groups; Reviewing alternative record keeping and assessment materials and procedures. (Collected from other schools and LEAs by assessment co-ordinator, plus published schemes such as PLeR {Primary Learning Record}.)
2.00 pm	Whole staff discussion of materials etc.
2.30 pm	Tea.
2.45 pm	in Curriculum teams: what implications are there for our curriculum area?
3.00 pm	Whole group to draw together team discussion and outcome, and to formulate a set of proposals and recommendations for the policy writing group to take away in their rewrite of the policy statement.
3.25 pm	Evaluation of the day.
3.30 pm	End.

The key point to note in this programme is the use of a variety of activities, i.e. listening, working with materials, discussion, decision making, etc., and the attempt to establish a pace or dynamic throughout the day. If an external speaker is to be involved caution needs to be taken in inviting the right person for the input, for not all 'specialists' have the skills necessary to stimulate and interest groups of teachers. It is advisable to go for the 'tried and tested' or consult someone whose judgement and recommendations are to be trusted.

Preparation

Once the programme has been drafted the operation can move into the preparation phase which will already have been defined in the action plan. The principal features will include:

- book external speaker and arrange a briefing;
- finalise programme;
- notify all participants with outline of the day;
- write course materials;
- confirm room is available and plan seating;
- disseminate any pre-reading;
- book refreshments/lunch;
- compile tutors' notes.

Naturally the tasks that need to be done will be shared between the team organising the day and others might well be brought in to help at this stage.

The list above is self-explanatory apart, perhaps, for the last item 'tutors' notes', at which we'll take a closer look.

It is essential for the lead person, or persons, in an INSET or training situation to have a detailed set of notes for the whole of the session; they must know precisely *who* is doing *what*, *where*, and for *how long*. Having a programme prepared is not enough for the day to run smoothly and for the hoped for dynamic to be maintained.

The following format for tutors' notes, used widely by trainers, will provide an illustration of one way of doing this; it can, of course, be modified according to need. The process is simply to sketch out the framework of headings then work through the programme writing down as much or as little as is needed (see Figure 10.2).

In practice the 'notes' column would need to be more extensive but not ending up looking like a fully blown script, which isn't really necessary.

Leaders' INSET day notes				
Time	**Who**	**Activity**	**Resources**	**Notes**
9.00 am	Doris	Coffee	Urn etc.	Handouts for 1st activity
9.15 am	me	Introduction	Flip-chart	Check all have programme
9.25 am etc.	Suraj	Review	OHP, acetates	Keep him on time

Figure 10.2

Implementation

Given that the planning and preparation has been done thoroughly and in this kind of detail implementation should flow smoothly and be 'nerve' free.

However, the INSET leader may be going into the session with concerns over a number of issues, one of them being, 'the colleague who would rather not be there'.

There are no easy ways around this problem though what can help is to start the day by giving a clear outline of its purpose and the benefits that a successful outcome will have for everyone. However reluctantly some colleagues might be at the INSET day, through lack of interest in the theme or negative feelings arising from experiencing poorly run training in the past, once the day starts with an interesting and promising introduction they are more likely to become involved. If there is more than one 'difficult' person then ensure that they are separated for small group activities and each placed with an 'enthusiast'.

Timekeeping during a busy INSET day is of the essence and it is helpful when working with another to arrange that each keeps an eye on the clock while their partner is giving a presentation or leading a discussion. Furthermore it is vital to establish with visiting speakers exactly what their time slot is and to ensure they stick to it.

Evaluation

It is important that time is allowed at the end of the day to allow for a written evaluation to be made of the day. While it is rewarding and pleasurable to have positive feedback of what has been prepared and presented, the prime purpose of the evaluation is that it should lead to the development of even more effective training in the future. However the evaluation is formulated, tick boxes, score out of 10, smiling faces, etc., it should include the opportunity for participants to express constructive criticism while avoiding personalising their comments.

Figure 10.3 is a sample from a management training course that could be adapted.

Days 3 and 4 evaluation
Please give each activity a rating of 1 to 5 (1= low, 5= high) according to its usefulness to you, and any other comments will be helpful.

Activity   **Rating**   **Comments**

Assignment feedback _____

Staff development _____

School budgets _____

Dealing with conflict _____

Figure 10.3

As part of the evaluation process a useful strategy is to conduct a short debriefing with the team involved in presenting the session and noting what went well, and why, as well as analysing activities that didn't go too well. This can provide extremely valuable learning for those involved, and only then may the bottle of wine be removed from the fridge!

11 Becoming an appraiser

It will be assumed here that the reader will be familiar with the main features of the process and structure of teacher appraisal and will probably have been involved as an 'appraisee'. The issues that will concern us in this chapter are those that relate to the development of the skills of the appraiser; becoming an appraiser.

The deputy's role within the school's appraisal scheme is a crucial one and on which its success or failure will hang. Even in very small schools the number of teachers that will have to be appraised during the two-year appraisal cycle will be more than the head-teacher alone can tackle, or in fact under the regulations, be allowed to take on, and the load will be shared, inevitably, with the deputy. It has become apparent during the first couple of years of schoolteacher appraisal that in larger schools the complexity of the management of appraisal means that a lead person, or appraisal co-ordinator, has had to be designated. It seems likely that many deputies will find this new function written into their job descriptions in the future. Again in larger schools additional teachers have had to be involved as appraisers and it is clear that when this happens there is a need for someone within the organisation to be able to induct and mentor them in the role.

In becoming an effective and skilled appraiser there are a number of core features which we will look at in a sequential fashion as they appear in the appraisal process, thus:

- knowledge and understanding of the purpose of appraisal and the school's policy;
- the appraiser/appraisee relationship;
- the collection of data;
- classroom observation and feedback;
- interviewing;
- setting targets;
- writing appraisal statements.

In order to contextualise these aspects of the appraiser's role here is a brief reminder of the events which take place in the conventional appraisal process. The sequence of activities after the matching of appraisee and appraiser normally follows this pattern:

1. An initial meeting.
2. Self-appraisal by the appraisee.
3. Data collection by the appraiser.
4. Classroom/task observation.
5. Observation feedback.
6. Appraisal interview and target setting.
7. Writing draft statement.
8. Confirmation of final statement.
9. Follow up meetings during the remainder of the cycle.

There may be, according to individual circumstances, other meetings built into this programme through agreement between the two involved.

Knowledge and understanding of the purpose of appraisal

Deputies coming into the appraiser role for the first time will have to familiarise themselves with three important sets of information and guidance; the statutory aspects of the 1991 regulations for schoolteacher appraisal (which can be found in the DES circular 12/91), the procedural guide-lines published by the Local Education Authority and, crucially, the school's own Policy for Appraisal.

The most effective way of getting to grips with the school's policy is to initiate a review, take it apart and reassemble it. Of course, the school may not have an established policy, in which case the policy writing machinery can be put into action as has been described in previous chapters. If this has to be tackled then each component of the appraisal process, as listed in 1 to 8 above, will need to be clarified and the agreed procedures recorded. This could prove to be an unwelcome additional burden to everyone concerned and a short cut through this thicket could be to take the LEA's guide-lines and modify them according to the needs of the school.

The appraiser/appraisee relationship

In small primary schools the question of matching appraiser to appraisee can prove to be a sensitive issue for if there are to be only two appraisers, i.e. head and deputy, then the permutations of choice are extremely limited. This situation is in marked contrast to that of secondary schools having, maybe, 80 plus members of staff thus enabling a wide range of matching options to be made. One way for the primary school to ease this problem is to increase the number of appraisers by, say, designating one or two other experienced teachers to the role. This has been taken by a small number of schools to its logical conclusion of making everyone on the staff an appraiser with each having just one colleague to appraise.

However the pairing is done, and the agreed arrangements must be outlined as an item in the policy statement, the success of the process will depend on the establishment of a positive working relationship. This will be helped by the appraiser setting the initial meeting in a highly professional context and by making it clear that there are guide-lines set and that they intend to follow these throughout the time they will be acting as appraiser. They will also emphasise the strict confidentiality, which should be mutually respected, in which they will carry out their responsibilities.

The purpose of this initial meeting is to provide a framework for the appraisal process and to promote the confidence of both parties involved, it will have a range of items that must be discussed, clarified and agreed. Breaking down this broad purpose what will need to be dealt with is:

- Confirming of appraisee's understanding of the appraisal scheme.

- Clarifying the aims of appraisal in the school.

- The appraiser gaining greater understanding of the teacher's work context.

- Discussion of the appraisee's work with reference to:
  - job description/wider responsibilities;
  - implications of the SDP;
  - recent training/ INSET;
  - any previous appraisal.

- Agreeing the scope of the appraisal by focusing in on specific aspects of the appraisee's work.

- Negotiating and agreeing methods of information gathering through:
  - self-appraisal;
  - classroom observation;
  - data collection.

- Arranging details of classroom observation including preparatory and feedback meetings.

- Confirming the timetable for the process including date, time and venue for the appraisal interview and any other supplementary meetings

A well managed and thorough initial meeting should see the relationship firmly established on a professional footing, with an appraisee confident that there are going to be no 'surprises' in store for them. This, of course, is only the first step, as the relationship will have to be maintained over a lengthy period of time. The first phase of the process, i.e. from the initial meeting to a finalised appraisal statement, will take up a good six weeks and the full cycle spreads over two years. What then will help the appraiser sustain this positive beginning?

Confidentiality will have to remain unassailed and visible throughout. There must be no discussion, unless appraisee initiated, of issues arising from the appraisal such as targets, data gathered or progress, with a third party. The appraiser will not be able to discuss, apart from in very general terms, the progress of the appraisal even within the senior management team. Finally, the appraiser will do their utmost to keep to agreed meeting times and deadlines.

Data collection

Data collection concerns the information that is gathered by the appraiser, and with the full knowledge and agreement of the teacher being appraised, which does not come from classroom observation or the teacher's own self-appraisal. It can be an area of potential risk if not handled carefully and the school's guide-lines should contain clear instructions of how it is to be implemented.

As information gathering, other than that obtained through classroom observation, is not a statutory requirement why is so much emphasis placed on its importance? This is a question that might well be asked of the deputy either during appraisal policy writing or from an appraisee during the initial meeting so an examination of the rationale behind this aspect of the process could prove helpful.

Purposes of data collection

- Provides information of the teacher's work outside the classroom.

- Highlights appraiser's specific whole-school responsibilities.

- Enhances appraiser's awareness of a wider context.

- Provides evidence for a non-classroom focus on which the appraisee may wish to have constructive feedback.

This can be illustrated using a common focus for appraisal, that of *the teacher's work as a curriculum co-ordinator*. This is an aspect of their role for which data gathered through classroom observation will not be entirely appropriate. What would be of greater relevance would be gathering the views of colleagues working within that curriculum team or to analyse the organisation of resources or observe the teacher leading a curriculum team meeting.

Having given the rationale for the wider gathering of data there will, naturally, be circumstances where it will not be appropriate or necessary but these are likely to be in a minority of cases for when the benefits of developing a broader picture of the teacher's work is explained appraisees welcome the idea. Nevertheless it will be the appraiser's task to reassure the teacher of his/her rights of protection in the collection and storage of data, procedures which must be detailed in the school's policy statement. We will take a look at the fundamental principles which should frame this protection.

The notes for guidance given by the then DES in Circular 12/91, Annex A, gave quite specific and helpful advice on the collection and handling of data from sources other than classroom or task observation. It deals particularly with the gathering of information from a third party, or parties. For example, in the scenario given above with the teacher's role as a curriculum co-ordinator being the focus, the appraiser may wish to seek information by interviewing a colleague in the co-ordinator's team. The guidance for the appraiser advises that he/she:

- conducts any such interview on a 1:1 basis;

- explains to the interviewee the purpose of the interview, and how the information will be treated;

- concentrates questioning on the agreed area of focus of the appraisal;

- puts the interviewee under no pressure, save that of relevance and accuracy;

- expects the interviewee to support general comments with specific examples;

- will expect the interviewee to discuss any significantly critical comments with the appraisee before they are used as appraisal information;

- will not accept any information received anonymously;

- does not behave in any way likely to threaten the trust and confidence upon which successful appraisal depends;

in addition it recommends that;

- 'Any written submissions should remain confidential to the author, the appraiser and the appraisee.'

- 'Those giving information should be encouraged to make fair and considered comments which they are prepared to acknowledge and to substantiate if required.'

It can be seen that behind the rather formal language the aim of this code of practice is to protect the integrity of the data collected and to safeguard the appraisee. They are a useful set of requirements to incorporate in the school's policy statement.

There are a number of ways in which additional information may be gathered, and the approach used will be determined largely by the agreed focus and constraints imposed by the organisation itself. The following information gathering strategies, together with their advantages and disadvantages, have been applied by appraisers in the recent past:

1. Task observation:
   For:
   - Useful for focusing on and giving feedback on specific features of appraisee's work.
   - Can lead to very specific targeted support.
   - Relatively cost effective, tending to be of finite, short activities.
   Against:
   - Takes appraiser away from their work.

- Needs careful planning.

2. Job shadowing:
   For:
   - Enables appraiser to get under the skin of someone's role.
   - Presents a holistic view as opposed to an observation snapshot.

   Against:
   - May present too broad a brushstroke.
   - Very costly in time.
   - Difficult to keep on focus.

3. Interviewing:
   For:
   - Reveals data not otherwise accessible.
   - Leads to enriched and informed feedback.
   - Enables the testing of appraisee's self-perceptions.
   - May help in developing appraisee's self image.

   Against:
   - Needs skilful handling.
   - May be threatening.
   - Interviewees require detailed briefing.
   - Time consuming.

4. Questionnaires:
   For:
   - Provides a quick overview.
   - Relatively easy to implement.
   - Enables a wide cross section of views to be gathered.

   Against:
   - Difficult to monitor the accuracy of responses.
   - Individual interpretation of questions may lead to spurious or inaccurate data.

It will be for the appraiser and the teacher to be appraised to negotiate and agree on the approach to be adopted, with the appraiser ensuring that the appraisee is completely comfortable with the method to be used and is clear about its implementation.

Classroom observation

This aspect of the appraiser's role was dealt with in considerable detail in Chapter 9 (page 113), and the principles, strategies and techniques described there apply equally well to this aspect of the appraisal process. Just a few reminders are necessary at this point.

First, classroom observation is a statutory part of school teacher appraisal and whatever the focus that has been agreed between appraiser and appraisee, and however distanced that focus is from classroom practice or management, it has to be undertaken. Deputies will be familiar with the regulations which stipulate that:

> 'School teachers should normally be observed teaching for a total of at least one hour, spread over two or more occasions.'

It is also well to remind ourselves that there are three components in classroom observation which have to be managed:

1. The preparatory meeting.
2. The classroom observation.
3. The feedback.

The appraisal interview

The appraisal interview is the time when all aspects of the appraisal process, self-appraisal, data gathering, classroom and task observation are drawn together to feed a discussion between the two teachers concerned. The outcome of this meeting will provide the substance of an appraisal statement, a set of targets and an action plan. It is at the core of teacher appraisal and its effectiveness, both in planning and implementation, will determine the success, or otherwise, of the whole process. Appraisees attach enormous importance to the event and have high expectations of its outcome; it is the appraiser's duty to see these are fulfilled

The remainder of this section will deal with the management of the interview:

1. The content.
2. The structure.
3. Management skills check-list.

The content of the interview

The content of the interview may well be predetermined by school policy which, if this is the case, could need clarification to enable a common understanding. For example, the staff may have agreed, in general terms, that the interview must cover:

1. A general focus.
2. A specific focus.

3. A whole-school focus.

The meat of the content needs to deal with concrete aspects of the appraisal process which the appraiser and appraisee have experienced. The discussion might be focused on:

- referring to the job description;
- appraisee's self appraisal;
- classroom observation notes;
- information gathered throughout data collection;
- task observation record;
- previous appraisal targets.

The structure of the interview

The interview should be planned well in advance to take on board:

1. An appropriate *meeting framework*, i.e. to have a clear beginning, middle and end which facilitates good communication.

2. The agreed *content*.

3. The construction of the *draft statement* to include the identification of professional development needs, target setting and action planning.

Deputies may wish to consider this agenda model for the meeting;

1. *Introduction*: welcome, clarification of purpose, agenda and procedures.

2. *General focus*: review of past year's work using job description and data collected.

3. *Specific focus*:
   - recognition of strengths, successes, constraints and concerns;
   - identification of need for support and development in relation to these and within the context of the School Development Plan;
   - discussion of career development needs.

4. *Conclusion*:
   - agreement on future development targets with related success criteria;
   - establishment of an action plan linked to SDP;

– summary of main points to be included in the appraisal statement.

Managing the interview: a check-list

- The setting:
  A quiet comfortable room away from interruptions, allowing adequate time (one and a half to two hours seems to be needed).

- The atmosphere:
  Friendly, relaxed, calm but professional.

- Approach:
  Through problem solving, negotiating targets and reaching agreement as to the way forward.

- Opening moves:
  Put the appraisee at ease, review the purpose of the interview and invite clarifying questions. Begin on a positive note or ask a straightforward first question.

- Middle:
  Keep to the agenda. Use summarising to move from discussion to target setting. Allow the appraisee to have the 'floor' – talking should be 80 per cent appraisee, 20 per cent appraiser!

- End:
  Review points agreed and check for agreement. Confirm arrangements for drafting and agreeing the statement and follow up meeting. Thank the appraisee for their co-operation.

Much of this will seem familiar to those deputies who will have been developing the skills and strategies of counselling and consultation and what was written in Chapter 9 should be applied during the appraisal interview.

Target setting

Of the many issues that have to be dealt with during appraisal training, target setting and writing will often produce the highest levels of anxiety and concern. Perhaps this is owing to the fact that many other aspects of the appraisal process are in some ways familiar and are extensions of teaching skills and approaches. Targeting, however, presents itself as something new and not within teachers' previous experience. The most effective way that trainers have in dealing with this apparent block is to demonstrate examples of targets that have been used in appraisal to show that they can be structured and written in a straightforward uncomplex fashion and should not be the cause of undue worry. The targets themselves, together with an action plan, date for completion and success criteria, will have been agreed during the appraisal interview but the appraiser will be left with the task of tidying up these agreements and recording them in some permanent form. The first step is for the school to decide on a common format for the recording of targets. This may be a home-made proforma or, more usually, a model that the LEA has developed for schools to use, either way the document will be incorporated into the set of documents that accompany the school policy.

The recording sheet will be likely to have the headings shown in Figure 11.1.

Targets	Action strategies	Resources	Completion date	Success criteria

Figure 11.1

The column headed 'Targets' will describe the nature of the agreed targets, which experience has shown will be limited to one major long-term objective together with perhaps two medium- or short-term tasks.

'Action strategies' will contain the approaches that the teacher will take along the road to reaching the target.

'Resources' might include, time or material and training costs that are likely to be needed.

The ' Completion date' needs to be realistic and not too specific, ie. 'The end of Spring Term 199–'

'Success criteria' will list the observable or measurable evidence that tells the teacher and appraiser that the target has been reached.

The example of a target for a primary curriculum co-ordinator shown in Figure 11.2 shows how this format can be applied.

1. *Target*: to improve the effectiveness of curriculum team meetings.

2. *Action strategies*:
   - Observe good practice in other curriculum teams;
   - Experiment with different meetings formats;
   - Seek advice of advisory teacher;
   - Take up place on curriculum co-ordinators management course.

3. *Resources*:
   - non contact time;
   - cost of course from INSET fund (£240 and supply cover).

4. *Completion date*: End of Autumn Term 199–.

5. *Success criteria*:
   - evaluation questionnaire to be compiled with appraiser for completion by curriculum team and SMT.
   - qualitative comparison of meeting outcomes now against those at the end of the target period.

Figure 11.2

Finally a reminder that targets should always aim to be SMART:

Specific, **M**easurable, **A**ttainable, **R**ealistic, **T**ime constrained

Statement writing

Statement writing can be a difficult and time consuming task for the appraiser and everything possible must be done through the school's agreed procedures to lessen the burden.

Again, as in target writing, a clear, uncluttered common format for the statement is essential. A broad agreement on style and presentation may also be of help to statement writers, for example: how formal/informal, appraisees to be referred to by first name or not, typed or handwritten?

The appraisal statement will have to contain certain core elements in order to represent accurately the process that the appraisee has experienced and these will include the following:

1. Personal information, i.e. names of the two involved, date of the interview.

2. Areas of agreed focus; to include personal focus and whole-school focus.

3. Details of current or recent professional development.

4. Sources of information collected, i.e. through classroom/task observation, peer interviews, etc. (though *not* the information itself).

5. Summary of the appraisal interview, including the agreed outcomes and directions to be taken by the appraisee. The targets themselves needn't be written here for they will already be detailed on the separate target proforma.

6. Space for the appraisee to add their own comments.

It is strongly recommended that the appraiser tackles the statement writing as soon as is possible after the interview in order to summarise the meeting with any degree of accuracy. The draft statement can be discussed with the appraisee and any factual inaccuracies corrected before the final version is presented to the teacher. He/she then has a statutory period of 20 days in which to register any complaints in regard to either the content of the statement or to the way in which the appraisal process was conducted. Deputies involved as appraisers are strongly recommended to familiarise themselves with both the statutory complaint procedures together with any local, LEA procedures. When the statement has been finalised it is a requirement that all documents produced during the appraisal period, i.e. classroom observation notes, data collected from colleagues, interview notes, etc., be destroyed.

Naturally this is not the end of the appraiser's task, for over the whole remaining period of the appraisal cycle they will be keeping a watching brief over the appraisee and will have arranged a series of meetings to review progress towards the targets and, in some cases, amending a target or shifting completion dates.

Appendices

Appendix I
Little Venice Primary School
Application for post of deputy

Job specification
Essential criteria

    E1   To have had a minimum of five years' experience as a successful primary classteacher.

    E2   To be able to express informed views on current issues in education.

    E3   To have read, and be willing to implement, the school's Equal Opportunities Policy.

    E4   To have management responsibility for at least one major curriculum area and to have an in-depth knowledge of its Programme of Study and Attainment Targets.

    E5   To be an effective communicator; both oral and written.

    E6   To have experience in organising and delivering INSET and staff development.

E7   To be an effective team worker.
E8   To show an understanding of working with parents and to be able to talk confidently to both large and small groups of adults.
E9   To be able to demonstrate an understanding of the governors' responsibilities.
E10   To have had experience in liaising with external agencies such as the educational psychologist, the police, community groups etc.

Appendix II
A policy for school policies – Copenhagen Primary

Statement of aims
A policy should be a tool to improve the quality of children's learning by ensuring continuity and consistency.
Equal opportunities
Policies should allow prospective, and new members of staff access to agreements already made in the school.
   Policies should make teaching expectations clear, so that staff can operate within them.
Assessment (success criteria)
Will new staff understand what is expected of them?
Will the policy lead to action ?
Practices
   1. The staff as a whole should decide on what policies are needed in the school and the appropriate timescale.

   2. Policies should be drafted and written by the appropriate curriculum or management team, or postholder, before being presented to the rest of the staff.

   3. The timescale will depend on the nature of the subject and whether it should be classified as 'contentious' or, 'non-contentious' according to the extent to which there is major disagreement or dissatisfaction with existing or proposed practice.

   4. All policies should be written originally in draft form and there must be adequate time for consultation in different forums with, when necessary, refinements before they are finalised

   5. A policy should not be more than two sides of A4 paper, typed.

   6. It should express base-line agreements which become non-negotiable until the policy is reviewed.

   7. It should be written without jargon and under these headings:

       a) Statement of aims.
       b) Equal opportunities.
       c) Health and safety (where appropriate).
       d) Time and weight in the curriculum.
       e) Assessment (including success criteria).
       f) Agreed practice (specific baseline expectations).

g) Resources (agreed organisation, roles, etc.).
h) Date of staff agreement.
i) Date and procedures for review.

Date of staff agreement ....

Date for review ....

Appendix III
Physical Education Policy – Copenhagen Primary

Satement of aims

1. To develop:
   a) physical skills, awareness, control and confidence.
   b) fitness with regard to strength, mobility and stamina.
   c) co-operation and competitive spirit.
   d) physical expression and creativity.

2. To allow children to experience and enjoy a wide range of physical experiences and activities.

3. To encourage children to discover, develop, enjoy and take a pride in their physical talents.

Equal opportunities
Teachers should be aware of the needs of individuals and groups of children so that all are given the opportunity to both experience different activities and to achieve success. In PE this has particular relevance to the stereotyped roles of gender, race, religion, culture and class in the choice of different activities and the clothing needed for them; understanding that health and safety of the children must be paramount.

Teachers must also be sensitive to those children at either end of the success scale, or who have physical or emotional special needs in PE.

Health and safety
The health and safety of the children is the direct responsibility of the teacher supervising the class and must be the first consideration in respect to discipline, content, equipment, clothing and jewellery.

Children should never be allowed on the gym apparatus without the direct supervision of a qualified teacher, or if wearing trousers or shoes.

Both the space being used and the apparatus must always be checked before allowing children to begin an activity.

In gymnastics, children should never help others by supporting them, unless they have been directly taught so to do and their ability is such that the teacher has decided it is safe. Crash mats should be used when specifically needed to practice an activity. They should not be used where they may encourage children to attempt activities beyond their capabilities or to cushion a jump from a height.

The older children use the Cally pool for swimming where an instructor and life-guard are provided. However, it is the teacher's responsibility to ensure that the situation is safe for the children at all times, i.e. that the staff are on duty etc.

Time and weight in the curriculum

Children at all ages at the nursery and primary school should have some kind of planned physical activity four times a week. The content of this should be varied, appropriate to the age of the children, be kept fairly short and be clearly physical and active.

Assessment

Assessment should be in the context of the aims of the lesson and relative to the skills being taught. It should take the form of:

1. Records of the content of the lessons in the class record book.

2. A summary of the child's progress over the year in different skills relating to aims.

3. Self-assessment by children relating to success criteria or objectives and goals set by the teacher.

Practice

1. Lessons should be short, controlled and with clear aims.

2. All children should be active for as much of the lesson as is possible. Instructions should be kept to a minimum and the lesson and apparatus should be organised so that children do not have to queue.

3. Lessons should include:
   – warm-up activities;
   – direct skills teaching;
   – the opportunity to explore, practice and use these skills;
   – hard cardio-vascular activity.

4. The elements of competition and performance should be addressed in order to build in success criteria for the children.

5. At an appropriate level children should experience:
   – gymnastics – skill-based creative work;
   – creative/expressive movement – drama or music based;
   – games – skill-based competitive or co-operative;
   – swimming – for older children.

6. If you have a child who is not taking part in the lesson because of illness or injury, try to give him or her a role, i.e. looking out for children who answer the task well, or

counting the number of times children knock into each other, etc. If a child is not taking part for any negative reason, forgotten kit, undisciplined behaviour, etc., they should not be in the hall or playground at all. They should be set work to do and sent to another class to finish that work.

Resources
There is fixed and free-standing gymnastics apparatus in both the lower and middle halls. There is a PE trolley, with a range of games equipment that can be used in the lower hall or wheeled outside. Teachers are responsible for ensuring that equipment is returned to the trolley after its use.

The resources team is responsible for ordering new equipment so please report any shortages to them.

Staff agreement: Spring Term 1992

Policy review: Spring Term 1993

Appendix IV
Model framework for job descriptions

(What follows is not specific to any particular post but some examples of content have been given where this helps clarification; with modification the format can be usefully applied to teachers other than the deputy.)

Name: **Date:** i.e. when post taken up

                                   Review date:

School:
Post held:–
– Deputy head with responsibilties defined below.
– Phase leader for infant classes.
– Curriculum leader for maths.

Salary scale:
General duties: these describe the tasks, responsibilities and duties common to all teachers in the school with reference to the nationally agreed Conditions of Employment of Teachers. Reference could be made to the use of directed and non-directed time, attendance required at staff meetings, parents meetings and other non-teaching commitments.

Specific duties:
1. As deputy head: here are the core duties and responsibilities specific to the deputy's role, they will vary according to local circumstances and needs. These may be usefully prefaced with an extract from the Conditions of Employment of teachers document which refers to deputies. 'A person appointed deputy headteacher in a school, in addition to carrying out the professional duties of a school teacher, including those duties assigned to them by the headteacher, shall:

1. assist the headteacher in managing the school or such part of as may be determined by the headteacher;

2. undertake any professional duty of the headteacher which may be delegated to them by the headteacher;

3. undertake, in the absence of the headteacher and to the extent required by them or their employers, the professional duties of the headteacher;

4. be entitled to a break of reasonable length in the course of each school day.'

An itemised agenda of specific duties then follows, these examples have been taken from a selection of job descriptions:

- 'To deputise for the head, in all respects, whenever they are absent from the premises.'
- 'To co-ordinate the school's curriculum and, in partnership with the head, to evaluate and monitor its effectiveness.'
- 'To participate in residential school journeys.'
- 'To be responsible for the general stock order.'
- 'To co-ordinate the work of the reception, Y1 nad Y2 teachers to ensure consistency, continuity and progression in teaching and learning in those classes.'
- 'To oversee and co-ordinate the work of curriculum leaders.'
- Etc.

2. As curriculum leader for maths: this would list the duties and requirements of a maths post holder and include items such as:

- Ensuring the development and implementation of the school's maths policy.
- Monitoring the delivery of maths throughout the school and ensuring it matches the requirements of the National Curriculum.
- Ordering, organising and monitoring of maths resources throughout the school.
- Organising and delivering maths INSET, staff meetings and workshops.
- Etc.

To whom responsible: headteacher.

Responsible for:

- The teaching and non-teaching staff working with reception, Y1 and Y2 classes.
- Those teachers having curriculum leadership responsibilities.
- In the absence of the head, all teaching and non-teaching staff of the school.

Agreed and signed:
Head:...
Deputy:......................................
Date:...

Appendix V
A self-perception inventory for use in team building

This has been taken from Belbin's *Management Teams: Why they Succeed or Fail* (1981).

Directions

1. For each section distribute a total of ten points among the statements that you think best describe your behaviour. These points may be distributed among as many statements as you like: in extreme cases they might be spread among all the statements, or ten points may be given to a single statement.
2. Enter the points in the table that appears after the last section of statements.

The statements

1. **What I believe I can contribute to a team:**
   a) I think I can quickly see and take advantage of opportunities.
   b) I can work well with a wide range of people.
   c) Producing ideas is one of my natural assets.
   d) My ability rests in being able to draw people out whenever I detect they have something of value to contribute to group objectives.
   e) My capacity to follow through has much to do with my personal effectiveness.
   f) I am ready to face temporary unpopularity if it leads to worthwhile results in the end.
   g) I can usually sense what is realistic and likely to work.
   h) I can offer a reasoned case for alternative courses of action without introducing bias or prejudice.

2. **If I have possible shortcomings in teamwork, it could be that:**
   a) I am not at ease unless meetings are well structured and controlled and generally well conducted.
   b) I am inclined to be too generous towards others who have a valid viewpoint that has not been given a proper airing.
   c) I have a tendency to talk too much once the group gets onto new ideas.
   d) My objective outlook makes it difficult for me to join in readily and enthusiastically with colleagues.

e) I am sometimes seen as forceful and authoritarian if there is a need to get things done.

f) I find it difficult to lead from the front, perhaps because I am over-responsive to group atmosphere.

g) I am apt to get too caught up with ideas that occur to me and so lose track of what is happening.

h) My colleagues tend to see me as worrying unnecessarily over detail and the possibility that things may go wrong.

3. **When involved in a project with other people:**
   a) I have an aptitude for influencing others without pressurising them.
   b) My general vigilance prevents careless mistakes and omissions being made.
   c) I am ready to press for action to make sure that the meeting does not waste time or lose sight of the main objective.
   d) I can be counted on to contribute something original.
   e) I am always willing to back a good suggestion in the common interest.
   f) I am keen to look for the latest in new ideas and developments.
   g) I believe my capacity for judgement can help to bring about the right decisions.
   h) I can be relied upon to see that all the essential work is organised.

4. **My characteristic approach to group work is that:**
   a) I have a quiet interest in getting to know my colleagues better.
   b) I am not reluctant to challenge the views of others or to hold a minority view myself.
   c) I can usually find a line of argument to refute unsound propositions.
   d) I think I have a talent for making things work once a plan has to be put into operation.
   e) I have a tendency to avoid the obvious and to come out with something unexpected.
   f) I bring a touch of perfectionism to any job I undertake.
   g) I am ready to make use of contacts outside the group itself.
   h) While I am interested in all views I have no hesitation in making up my mind once a decision has to be made.

5. **I gain satisfaction in a job because:**
   a) I enjoy analysing situations and weighing up all the possible choices.
   b) I am interested in finding practical solutions to problems.
   c) I like to feel I am fostering good working relationships.
   d) I can have a strong influence on decisions.
   e) I can meet people who may have something new to offer.
   f) I can get people to agree on a necessary course of action.
   g) I feel in my element when I can give a task my full attention.
   h) I like to find a field that stretches my imagination.

6. **If I am suddeenly given a difficult task with limited time and unfamiliar people:**
   a) I would feel like retiring into a corner to devise a way out of the impasse before developing a line.
   b) I would be ready to work with the person who showed the most positive approach.
   c) I would find some way of reducing the size of the task by establishing what different individuals might contribute.
   d) My natural sense of urgency would help ensure that we did not fall behind schedule.
   e) I believe I would keep cool and maintain my capacity to think straight.
   f) I would retain a steadiness of purpose in spite of the pressure.
   g) I would be prepared to take a positive lead if I felt the group was not making progress.
   h) I would open up discussions with a view to stimulating new thoughts and getting something moving.

7. **With reference to the problems I am subject to when working in groups:**
   a) I am apt to show my impatience with those who are obstructing progress.
   b) Others may criticise me for being too analytical and insufficiently intuitive.
   c) My desire to be sure that work is properly done can hold up proceedings.
   d) I tend to get bored rather easily and rely on one or two stimulating members to spark me off.
   e) I find it difficult to get started unless the goals are clear.
   f) I am sometimes poor at explaining and clarifying complex points that occur to me.

g) I am conscious of demanding from others the things I cannot do myself.

h) I hesitate to get my points across when I run up against real opposition.

Points table

Statement					Responses			
	a]	b]	c]	d]	e]	f]	g]	h]
1								
2								
3								
4								
5								
6								
7								

Analysis sheet

1. Now transpose the scores from the points table above, entering them section by section in the table below.
2. Add up the points in each *column* to give a total team-role distribution score.

Statement	CW	CH	SH	PL	RI	ME	TW	CF
1	g....	d....	f....	c....	a....	h....	b....	e....
2	a....	b....	e....	g....	c....	d....	f....	h....
3	h....	a....	c....	d....	f....	g....	e....	b....
4	d....	h....	b....	e....	g....	c....	a....	f....
5	b....	f....	d....	h....	e....	a....	c....	g....
6	f....	c....	g....	a....	h....	e....	b....	d....
7	e....	g....	a....	f....	d....	b....	h....	c....
Totals	—	—	—	—	—	—	—	—

The highest scoring team role will indicate how best you can make your mark in a management or project team. The next highest scores can denote back-up team roles towards which you should shift if for some reason there is less group need for your primary role.

The two lowest scoring in team roles imply possible areas of weakness. But rather than attempting to reform in this area, you may be better advised to seek a colleague with complementary strengths.

Full descriptions of the team roles are given in Chapter 6.

Appendix VI – Kolb's experiential learning cycle

A theory of adult learning which is widely subscribed to holds that competence and learning is developed by repeatedly going around an experiential learning cycle. This idea, illustrated below, was developed by the psychologist David Kolb.

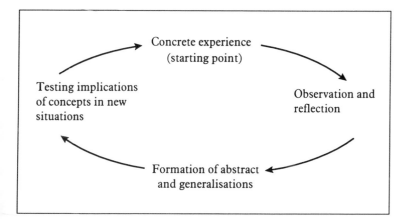

In order to make sense of experience we need to think and reflect on it. This allows the concrete experience to be assimilated into our sets of concepts and patterns of behaviour. Further testing and experimenting with this new learning will refine and develop our understanding of the concepts.

Further reading

Belbin, M. (1981) *Management Teams: Why They Succeed or Fail*, London: Heinemann.

Bond and Feletti (1986) *Understanding and Facilitating Adult Learning*, London: Kogan Paul.

Caldwell, B. J. and Spinks, J. M. (1988) *The Self-Managing School*, Lewes: Falmer Press.

Craig, I. (1987), *Primary School Management in Action*, Harlow: Longman.

Coulson, A. and Cox, M. (1975) 'What do deputies do?' *Education 3–13*, **3**, 2, 100–103.

Davies, B. and Ellison, L. (1990) *Education Management for the 1990s*, Harlow: Longman.

Delaney *Primary School Staff Appraisal*, Harlow: Longman.

DES (1992) *Curriculum Organisation and Classroom Practice in Primary Schools*. A discussion paper. Alexander, R., Rose, J. and Woodhead, C.

Everard K. B. and Morris G. (1990) *Effective School Management*, London: Paul Chapman.

Glatter, B., Preedy, M., Riches, C. and Masterton, M. (1988) *Understanding School Management*, Milton Keynes: Open University Press.

Handy, C. and Aitkin, R. (1986) *Understanding Schools as Organisa-*

tions, Harmondsworth: Penguin.

Hargreaves, D. and Hopkins, D. (1991) *The Empowered School*, London: Cassell.

Harvey, (1994) 'Empowering the Primary School Deputy Principal', *Educational Management and Administration*, 22.

Holly, P. and Southworth, G. (1989) *The Developing School*, Lewes: Falmer Press

Lane, P. *If it Moves*, NAHT.

ILEA (1985) *Improving Primary Schools*. Report of the Committee on Primary Education.

Mortimer, P., Sammons, P., Stoll, L., Lewis, D. and Ecob, R. (1988) *School Matters*, London: Open Books.

Murgatroyd, S. and Morgan, C. (1993) *Total Quality Management and the School*, Milton Keynes: Open University Press.

Southworth, G. (ed.) (1987) *Readings in Primary School Management*, Lewes: Falmer Press.

Taylor, W. (1992) *Coverdale on Management* London: Butterworth Heinemann.

Welsh HMI (1985) *Leadership in Primary Schools, HMI Wales Occasional Paper*, DES Welsh Office.

Index